CHARLIE
A GOLDEN MEMORY

South Carolina Society Hall
(Watercolor by Paul Hogarth, R.A.)

CHARLESTON
A Golden Memory

by
Charles Anderson

Illustrations by
Paul Hogarth

Wyrick & Company

Published by Wyrick & Company
12 Exchange Street
Charleston, SC 29401

Copyright © 1992 by Charles R. Anderson
All rights reserved

Printed in the United States of America
designed by Linda Blackwell

Library of Congress Cataloging-In-Publication Data
Anderson, Charles Roberts, 1902-
Charleston, a golden memory / by Charles Anderson;
illustrations by Paul Hogarth.
p.   cm.
ISBN 0-941711-18-8

1. Charleston (S.C.) – Description and travel.
2. Charleston (S.C.) – Social life and customs.
3. Anderson, Charles Roberts, 1902-
– Homes and haunts – South Carolina – Charleston.
I. Title.

F279.C44A5 1992   975.7'915–dc20   91-42708
CIP

Cover illustration by Paul Hogarth, R.A.:
Dock Street Theater and St. Philip's Church

Contents

To My Muses
Thalia (Eugenia Blount)
and
Clio (Mary Pringle)

Foreword

This is not a history of Charleston. It is my memory of experiences there half a century ago during a year-long visit, so joyous I want to share them. Remembering, consisting chiefly of impressions, is not notable for accuracy of detail. When my narrative involves matters of historical record, I have tried to correct my lapses of memory. What errors remain will be overlooked, I hope, by those who enjoy these impressions — my real purpose in this reminiscence.

All memory is a form of fiction.

Over the years, everything changes — if it's alive. Over the time-span of fifty years, a city can change beyond recognition — if it gives in to the pressures of progress. Especially a place like Charleston, whose grandeur is so fragile. But in any civilized society there are traditional forces that tend to slow the pace of change in order to preserve the best of a cherished heritage, even while sharing in a new prosperity. Native Charlestonians, newcomers, and visitors today may use these memoirs to measure the transformation of this unique American city during the past fifty years. Can Charleston, as well as Paris, boast:

La plus ça change, la plus c'est la même chose?

The more it changes, the more it's the same thing? Or does Old Charleston survive only as a show-place for tourists?

CHARLESTON:
A GOLDEN MEMORY

The Way It Was, Then

About seven in the morning, after a cup of strong black coffee, we would mount our bikes and roll down Elliott Street to East Battery. Turning south, we would pedal slowly past Rainbow Row to enjoy the early light on these tall merchants' houses, newly restored some fifty years ago. At that date such bright colors were unique in Charleston. Most of its old houses were either mildewed tabby or genteel shabby. "Too poor to paint, too proud to whitewash," was the local quip.

Back in 1938 the colors, like the traffic noises, were much quieter. Charleston was a peaceful city, what developers would call "sleepy." The special charm of these early morning rides was the peace, and the subdued colors. As we drifted down East Battery, the more impressive three- and four-storied mansions of the late 18th and early 19th centuries loomed up, with their elegant piazzas overlooking walled gardens, facing south to catch the breeze. The love of privacy complements the love of peace. Just beyond the Carolina Yacht Club, we wheeled up onto the High Battery for a double vantage point. To the right we could catch a glimpse into those gardens. To the left, dawn was coming up over Fort Sumter, tinting the harbor with pastels. Then swinging around the Boulevard, we dismounted at the Fort Sumter Hotel and walked our bikes along the oyster-shell paths through White Point Gardens — laid out exactly one hundred years earlier as the most distinctive feature of Charleston's topography — to watch the first golden glints of a new day filter through the canopy of live oaks hung with Spanish moss.

Mounting again, we pedalled down South Battery past those houses that commanded such a grand view of the waterfront. From this point we could choose any one of several rewarding routes through the old residential quarter: Up Church Street to Atlantic, across to Meeting, up that handsome street to Tradd, over to Legare Street, back down to South Battery, then west over to Ashley River, and along Broad Street toward home — for a typical ride. At this time of morning, back then at the end of the Great Depression, you had a feeling of being in the 18th century. Almost no cars on the street, either parked or moving; the old ones had gone to their reward, and few people had money to spare for new ones. The buzz of renewed prosperity had not come yet, so there were not even many pedestrians stirring. An occasional shopkeeper on the way to open up, a cook or yardman arriving to start things going in one of the big houses. But for the most part all was peace and quiet. Once in a while the silence was broken by the sing-song of a street-crier:

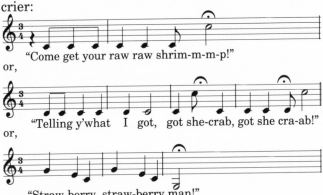

"Come get your raw raw shrim-m-m-p!"

or,

"Telling y'what   I   got,   got she-crab, got she cra-ab!"

or,

"Straw-berry, straw-berry man!"

depending on the season.

Half a century ago Charleston was a peaceful city all day long, and the only horse-drawn (or mule-drawn) vehicles were the hucksters' wagons. As we drew close to home about eight o'clock, a whiff of breakfast bacon or coffee brewing sharpened our appetites. Down St. Michael's Alley and the long block of Elliott brought us to No. 5. Through the gate and into the garden where Lucile, of blessed memory, had breakfast all ready for us on the terrace. If the shrimp man had come to our door that morning, we would have the Charleston special: biscuits, hominy, and shrimp broiled in butter. He sold shrimp by the "plate-ful," a marvelously unstandardized way of measuring. If you were a good customer it was piled high; if a poor one, just enough shrimp to cover the plate.

Breakfast in the garden, a dream of Eden! And I seem to remember having breakfast there through the year. ("Speak, Memory! Was everything, including the weather, better fifty years ago? Or am I falling into that trap of the-good-old-days?") Anyhow, on this heavenly October day back then we lingered long over our coffee among the flowers. A capacity for leisure goes quite naturally with a sense of privacy and a love of peace.

Stirring himself at last, the "ten-o'clock-scholar" gathered his notes and papers together and set off for the Charleston Library Society a few blocks away on King Street, brief case in one hand and in the other a bunch of roses, or whatever bouquet the garden offered, for Miss Ellen FitzSimons. A tiny fragile-looking creature, cricket-like in her chirping, bright-eyed and busy as a bee in her beloved garden of books. Miss Ellen was not only the librarian but *the* library, presiding over her treasured archives with a fierce and possessive love.

"What will it be this morning?" she asked with genuine interest, because my research project was one dear to her heart.

"Grayson's little volumes of verse, please. *The Country, The Hireling and the Slave*, and anything else you can find."

"Good. He needs dusting off!" So began my long day's labor — a labor of love really — from 10 to 2 p.m., four hours being long enough to lose oneself back into the past. I was doing research for a book to go with the title staring at me from my typewriter: "A Literary History of Charleston, 1760-1860." This was my professional justification for spending a sabbatical year in Charleston, on leave-of-absence from Duke University. I had won a Rosenwald Fellowship, with a generous grant of $2,000. Together with $1,800, my half-salary from Duke, our income for the year would be $200 larger than usual. We felt comfortably rich, and happy, as we looked forward to our free year.

1

Discovering Old Charleston

We were driving down King Street on the afternoon of our arrival in Charleston, when our eye was caught by an anomaly. Several jewelry stores, banks, and other businesses had clocks for their signs. One of them said 20 minutes to 3, another half-past 11, a third 7 o'clock, a fourth noon, and finally 5:15.

"This is the city for me!" Eugenia cried out with joy. "No back talk from the clock!"

Freed from the restrictions of clock time, we arrived nevertheless just in time to watch the sunset from our room at the Fort Sumter Hotel. We were allowing ourselves this luxury, one night only, for romantic reasons. In 1935, we had spent the last glorious days of our honeymoon here, made memorable by a little event. I had been planning to buy Genie a very particular gift to commemorate our wedding trip, and Charleston was just the place to find it. But how can a groom slip away from his bride? The opportunity came up unexpectedly the first morning, when she discovered that a stone was loose in the diamond cluster of her engagement ring (the same ring my grandfather had given to his bride in 1865).

"I'll rush it up to a jeweler while you take your bath," I promised and dashed out.

There was a traffic cop at the corner of South Battery and King, so I pulled up alongside and asked where I could find a store with antique jewelry for sale.

"Your best bet is Adams & Ortman, straight up King Street," was the reply, and there I went.

They produced exactly what I was looking for, a pair of Victorian solid-band gold bracelets, delicately chased. But they looked so small! Suppose they wouldn't fit?

"I wonder if I could just show them to my wife" — I stumbled over that word, in spite of rehearsals — "and see if they are, well, suitable; I could leave a deposit."

"No need for that," he replied quietly: "Just take them down to the hotel and if your bride likes them come back and we can settle."

Bride! How did he know *that*? And how did he know he could trust me, a stranger? He just smiled courteously.

They did fit, and Genie was ecstatic. We returned together, so the jeweler could adjust the snap-fasteners. Now time to pay.

Taking him to one side I whispered, "You've been so kind, I wonder if I can pay half of the $100 in cash, and give you a check for the rest?" This was the first honeymoon I'd been on, and I didn't want my cash to run out.

"No problem," he said. "Make the check for the full amount and keep your cash for an emergency."

None of that parrot talk, "Have a nice day," thank God. He had already given us a lovely one. No wonder we fell in love with Charleston. Manners before money. (In my excitement I'd forgotten all about the ring. I fished it out of my pocket and he tightened the loose stone. No charge!)

Now, three years later in the same hotel room, this memory came flooding back when Genie clinked her gold bracelets together, saying: "Maybe this is why I wanted to come back, to bring them home for a visit. I'd love to meet the dear old lady who had to sell them. Maybe she'd enjoy wearing them again for a spell." Such endearing aspects of Charleston were certainly part of our pleasure in coming back. The next day we looked around for a cheaper hotel than the Fort Sumter, since it might take a week or so to find just the right house to rent for our academic year on leave. Charleston had only a limited offering of hotels back then. For us the Timrod Hotel seemed rather run-down, and the Francis Marion a bit far from the center of things. We settled happily for the Brewton Inn, an old house turned hostel at the corner of Tradd and Church Streets, with rambling corridors and rooms on two sides of a courtyard. It was reasonable in price, and had all needed conveniences including a dining room.

(Now, for a classic touch of irony. On Meeting Street

just above Market stood for more than a century a truly grand hostelry, The Charleston Hotel, erected in 1838-39 at the peak of the city's ante-bellum prosperity and serving as the center of its civic life for decades. It was still there in 1905 when it received a rare encomium from one of its distinguished guests, the cosmopolite Henry James: "The Charleston Hotel had an appearance of 'dating', with its fine old neoclassic front, and of a certain romantic grandeur of scale; the scale positively of 'Latin' construction, in my vast saloon-like apartment, which opened to a high colonnade. The great canopied and curtained bed was really in the grand manner, and the ghost of a rococo tradition, the tradition of the transatlantic South, glimmered generally in the decoration. The place might have been a palace." (*The American Scene*) Over the years, this grand old Charleston Hotel was allowed to slip into such dilapidation it was razed to make way for an auto court, even before the tourist trade began to flourish. The Preservation Society, focused on saving old dwelling houses during its early years, was unable to rescue the old Charleston Hotel.)

Using the Brewton Inn as our base, we explored the old residential quarter for several days on our own, simply following up newspaper ads and posted signs "For Rent." Not too many possibilities showed up — this was years before the visitor flood began — and all we found were beyond our purse. An old carriage-house elaborately restored, a kitchen building in a back yard, or a two-story wing added at the rear of one of the big houses. Just the thing for a retired admiral, a wealthy sportsman wanting some sunshine and some good shoots on a nearby plantation, a good-sized family looking for a winter home. Having reached a dead end, we reluctantly turned to a real estate agency.

By a stroke of good luck we were put under the wing of Miss Kitty Hutson, a lady totally free of the aggressive traits all too common in that trade. She listened sympathetically to the paradox of our poetic desires and our prosaic purse, then without more ado took us straight away to 5 Elliott Street (formerly known as Poinsett's Alley after a Huguenot family that lived and prospered there). She opened the wrought iron gate and we walked down a narrow path to the brick terrace at the back, really the front, of the house. There we stood: before us a picture-book garden, and as we turned around a picture-book house, the clean simple lines of a small two-storied stuccoed house, which had been a linen shop in the 18th century with the owner's quarters above. Now restored as a four room house: a sizeable living/dining room with double French doors opening on the terrace; behind, on the street side, a small kitchen and the garage; upstairs two bedrooms with connecting bath, the larger one overlooking the garden. And each room had its own fireplace. We were enchanted! Our dream come true! As with all dreams we had to wake up. The asking price was $125 a month, which took too big a bite out of our budget. Miss Hutson promised to see what could be done. She would send a wire to the owner, a sculptress, who was still in New York, her Charleston winter having been canceled this year for business reasons. A few days later Miss Hutson showed us the good news in the form of a pair of telegrams.

"Nice young couple want to rent for 8 months. Can pay $100 but would prefer to pay less."

"Let 'em have it for $85." Graciousness had infiltrated the market place. Needless to say, we moved in promptly.

Kitty Hutson waved her magic wand twice more before she left us on our own. Asked if she knew where we could get a maid, she sent us Lucile, a cheerful, intelligent young black woman who soon became our good friend as well as a first-rate cook. So Genie, who was herself quite a gourmet in the kitchen, could also have a year's leave-of-absence. Then, the real surprise. Miss Hutson had also passed on word of us to her good friend Sam Stoney, who came to call before the week was out, and stayed to dinner. Samuel Gaillard Stoney was a gentleman of small stature, swarthy complexion ("All Gaillards tetched with the tar-brush," he laughed); looking a bit Mephistophelian (and occasionally acting the part) with his goatee, raised eyebrows, and slightly unruly hair; the most famous raconteur in Charleston and one of its most entertaining eccentrics — a brand new version of the man-who-came-to-dinner. Now we had a cook to prepare the meals and a dependable guest to help us eat them. In a manner of speaking we felt well established in Charleston, though we had not yet been taken in by the "establishment." That could come later. Our life was much too busy with settling in, and settling down, to have given any thought to moving up.

Typical of the little touches that made us contented with our situation in Charleston was this little incident: One morning as I stepped out of our gate, a gentleman coming down Elliott Street paused, raised his hat, and inquired if we were visitors. Learning we'd be here for the better part of a year, he said: "I'm sure you'll enjoy yourselves. Last place left a gentleman can live. Good day, sir."

Lucile was most helpful with practical information, where to find a department store, a five-and-dime, a hardware store. Fishmonger and butcher as well as fruit and vegetables, she said, can be found at the old open market; staples at Ohlandts nearby on Meeting Street. Supermarkets had not yet invaded the old city. Where could we buy two second-hand bicycles? Lucile knew, and soon we were mounted, not only for our early morning rides but for errands and such. While Genie added a few personal touches to the interior decor to give it her signature, I sat on a stool across the street making a pen-and-ink sketch of the lovely wrought-iron gate at No. 5 Elliott Street, with an admiring audience of several black boys and girls, children of our neighbors. When the drawing was finished I took it to the printer around the corner on Broad Street to make it into Christmas cards, and in a miniature version to be printed at the head of some note paper, for spreading our good news to family and friends. Believe it or not, this same establishment, Walker & Evans, had published the slender volumes of Timrod, Hayne, Grayson and other Charleston poets a century ago. Continuity keeps tradition alive!

No 5 Elliott St-Charleston S.C.

2

A Little Renaissance
In The 1930's

For cultural matters Sam Stoney was our friendly guide. A lucky strike for us because there was a lot going on at that time in literature and the arts, and Sam was a sort of presiding consciousness and ready commentator on all this activity, somewhat like the omniscient narrator in a Henry James novel. First of all Sam sponsored my application for membership in the Charleston Library Society, so my research project could get under way. He also introduced me to the Poetry Society of South Carolina, with which I was to have delightful associations. This organization had been formed in the 1920's shortly after Eliot and Pound had stirred up a poetic revolution in England as well as in America. The rebirth of literature in South Carolina was recorded annually in the *Year Book* of the Poetry Society, along with accounts of new activity in the fine arts. By the 1930's Charleston was enjoying a veritable renaissance with writers such as Josephine Pinckney, Dubose Heyward, and Hervey Allen. Not in the big league with Frost, O'Neill, Faulkner and Hemingway, perhaps. But there was something more than local celebrity in the sensitive poetry of Pinckney's *Sea-Drinking Cities* (1927), Heyward's *Porgy* as novel-play-opera (1925, 1927, 1935), and Allen's best-selling romance *Anthony Adverse* (1936).

Most exciting of all was the Carolina Art Association, a three part organization consisting of the Gibbes Art Gallery, the Dock Street Theater, and a press for publishing books on the arts, all under the energetic direction of Bob Whitelaw. We became "regulars" at the Gibbes, and were keenly interested in the Association's imprints. One of them was a gift to us by the author, *Plantations of the Carolina Low Country* (1938) by Samuel Stoney (in collaboration with Albert Simons); and two more were on the agenda by other Charleston friends we met as the year moved on. Finally, the Dock Street Theater, of special interest to Genie who had enjoyed a brief career with a repertory company in California. As one of the WPA projects in the early years of the Depression, the old Planter's Hotel on Church Street was transformed into the new Dock Street Theater, taking its name from the long defunct 18th century theater around the corner on Dock (now Queen) Street. The opening performance in 1935 was a repeat of Farquhar's *Recruiting Officer*, which had been presented when the original theater first opened in 1735. Continuity, even though picked up after a lapse of decades.

To get season tickets, we were told, I must go to the office of a local business man, Thomas Tobias. I was courteously received, and while we were leavening the business matter with a pleasant exchange, I couldn't help being struck by the photograph on his desk.

"May I ask," I hesitated, "well, that fabulously beautiful young lady looks so much like a former student of mine at the University of Georgia named Rowena Wilson."

"That was her name before she became my wife," he replied with the smile of one accustomed to such compliments.

There were six or eight plays during the season, new and old ones of the drawingroom comedy or romantic farce variety, acted with a real flair by an excellent amateur company boosted by an occasional lead from New York. We attended them all, and as subscribers were eligible for the receptions in the Green Room at intermissions, where we made some pleasant acquaintances — of a rather reserved sort, in the British manner.

With all these cultural activities open to us in this most civilized of small American cities, our life seemed full enough. We had arrived here without knowing a soul, and if Charleston's inner life was closed to outsiders that was quite understandable. It had the reputation of being snobbish, but to us it just seemed contented. And we were contented too. Sam Stoney could easily have opened the doors for us, but he didn't have the remotest idea who we *were,* so he skillfully kept our friendship on a jolly and animated but surface level, for the time being. Without knowing a soul? Well, there was an elderly Charleston lady whom I faintly remembered from my childhood, when she had been a neighbor and great friend of my mother during a residence of several years in Macon, Georgia. A letter from mother said we must call on Margaret Huger Kershaw, and after the proper preliminaries we knocked on the door of her fine old Church Street house.

Mrs. Kershaw was a tall and rather statuesque lady who wore her widow's weeds with a certain majesty, befitting her posture and her white hair. After reminiscences about "dear Gertrude" and the rest of my family, she inquired pleasantly about our plans, how long we were staying, and if we had found an agreeable place to live. When we spoke of our little house on Elliott Street, she adroitly skirted around that topic, saying: "When I was a young lady I always went down to Water Street before crossing over to East Battery and the harbor. Elliott Street in those days," she concluded with a delightful euphemism, "was entirely given over to sailors' boarding houses." We did our best to reassure her by saying that three other houses besides ours had been restored on Elliott Street, and all the rest were inhabited by very respectable black families.

(My memory of our pleasant relations with blacks in Charleston fifty years ago was confirmed by a letter

to the editor of the *News and Courier* in 1988. It was
written by Mr. Herbert Fielding, prominent black
business man and State Senator, to protest an edito-
rial which seemed to him "divisive and race-baiting."
This led him to a reminiscence about his boyhood in
downtown Charleston during the 1930's: "My friends
and I (black and white) shot marbles, rode skate-
mobiles and scooters throughout the neighborhood.
Blacks and whites lived next door to each other and
enjoyed and respected each other. In my travels in
America and abroad I have always felt proud of the
long-standing state of race relations in my home
town." Were race relations better fifty years ago than
they are today in "historic Charleston?" Ironically,
during the very decade of the Civil Rights Movement
Charleston became more and more segregated in the
matter of housing. As real estate values escalated,
many blacks were unable to afford the rising price of
houses in the old city and began moving north of Calhoun Street, and into the suburbs.)

When a week later we invited Mrs. Kershaw to tea
in our garden she accepted the challenge gaily. But
when she made her very first venture into the hazards
of Elliott Street she was accompanied by her large
family retainer Tina walking, not the usual two steps
behind, but in the vanguard to ward off any sailors
that might be reeling out of a girl friend's nest! When
I had delivered the tea invitation, by hand, I had
asked if by any chance I had left my hat there when

we first came to call. Tina handed it to me with an unexpected comment: "We sure enjoyed having it here. First time a gentleman hat on our hall table in I don't know when." Margaret Huger Kershaw, living alone with Tina in her peaceful shuttered old house, had apologized for being so out-of-things she wouldn't be able to do for us herself what she'd like to do, but would get in touch with a young cousin. It was not long before Miss Anna Rutledge came to call. One proper introduction and the doors began to open, even in a very private world. Charleston seemed "contented" to take us in.

We were not caught up in a social whirl, thank goodness. No welcoming reception, no unseemly haste. Slowly and pleasantly we were taken into old Charleston sufficiently to feel comfortably at home. As it turned out, Dr. Rutledge was not well at the time so Anna said her mother would have to postpone receiving us at "44" for several weeks — "44" being the Rutledge home on South Battery. Meanwhile her elderly cousins, Miss Caroline and Miss Alice Huger Smith, wished to do the honors by inviting us to lunch at their home on Church Street. This turned out to be an occasion of double delight. In addition to the quiet charm of two maiden lady hostesses presiding over a savory chicken dish, it proved to be our introduction to yet another phase of Charleston's renaissance, that of the creative arts. For Miss Alice was the most gifted of the current painters, sculptors, etchers, and woodblock artists in this remarkable little city. She had drawn the illustrations for her father D. E. Huger Smith's *Dwelling Houses of Old Charleston* (1917), also the watercolors for *A Carolina Rice Plantation of the Fifties* (1936), and a series of paintings of the marshes and rivers with their water fowl, wild flowers, and trees. She told us how she would get up before dawn and go out into the fields and swamps to wait for a blue heron or white ibis to rise from the grasses so she could sketch it taking flight, and make notes on the rapidly shifting colors at daybreak. Of special interest was her account of the new technique she was experimenting with: to collect pieces of driftwood and old cypress panelling, then study the shapes and grain of wood for suggestions of figure and pattern, finally to develop these possibilities in sculpture or painting. Listening to an artist talk so enthusiastically about the creative process was a real treat, coming unexpectedly as it did after this delightful little luncheon party.

Our discovery of Alice Smith-as-artist gave a new zest to our visits to the Gibbes Gallery, the Library, and book stores looking for some of her work to buy: the *Dwelling Houses* for example (which became our invaluable guide in prowling the old city), color prints when possible, or to see exhibits of originals. In the process we also discovered the other artists of that generation, though we did not have the privilege of becoming acquainted with them: Alfred Hutty's etchings, Willard Hirsch's sculptures, and especially the work of Elizabeth O'Neill Verner, Charleston's other leading artist. A handsome volume was published by her that year, *Prints and Impressions of Charleston* (1939), etchings picturing Charleston in the 1920's and 30's, with the artist's reminiscences by way of introduction. It was now clear that Charleston's little renaissance covered the whole range of the arts — including music, in a token way, with a burgeoning symphony orchestra and concerts of the Society for the Preservation of Spirituals, founded in the 1920's. An impressive volume, *The Carolina Low Country*, was published by the Society in 1931, with essays, poems, and pictures by members to provide the background for a selection of Spirituals. Nothing world-shaking about any of this. But it was all Charlestonian — artists, performers, audiences — ninety percent, at least.

Several volumes, contemporary with Charleston's little renaissance, were by older writers who tended to romanticize and sentimentalize the city and the Lowcountry, naturally enough. By the time of World War I it was clear that the old plantation way of life *1911* — which had struggled valiantly to survive for half a century after the Civil War and Emancipation — was doomed. The boll weevil brought an end to sea-island cotton, and rice culture had shifted to Louisiana because Carolina's Lowcountry was too marshy for planting and harvesting by machinery. The sense of loss, of realization by the older generation that a very special way of life was gone forever, dominated their writings. By the 1930's a younger generation was finding new things to say about Charleston: as creative writers, as artists, and as historians. This little renaissance gave a sense of reality and renewed vitality to the city we came to know in 1938-1939.

Anna Rutledge not only introduced us to the current artistic activity in Charleston but was herself deeply involved in its art history, having almost completed her landmark book *Artists in the Life of Charleston.* As in any proper renaissance, the resurgence of creative art is often accompanied by a revival of interest in the past, searching for links with a tradition. Anna was one of the young historians inspired by Laura Bragg, director of the Charleston Museum, all of them amateurs in the best Charlestonian sense of that word. A lady of about our age (and still a devoted friend after half a century), Anna might seem at first to be a Southern version of the Blue-Stocking in her dedication to all things cultural. But she differed strikingly from the New England stereotype in her graces as a hostess and her flair for exotic costumes, with turbans and scarfs and capes. Another of the amateur historians was her friend Kitty Ravenel, who became our friend too, author of *The Architects of Charleston*, an authoritative book that was also lucid and witty. She came from a writing family: her mother a poet and her grandmother the author of *Charleston:*

The Place and the People (1906), a pleasant volume that filled in the general historical background for visitors like us.

We were privileged to read both of our friends' books in typescript, several years before publication. Along with Stoney's book on the plantations, they fed back into my research project with an unexpected effect. I had been concerned for sometime lest my subject should prove too thin, by comparison with my first book that was being published this very winter, a full-scale interpretation of one of America's literary giants, Herman Melville. How could I work up a similar enthusiasm, and communicate it to lovers of literature, by writing a literary history of ante-bellum Charleston? Even its best writings — the poems of Henry Timrod and Paul Hayne, the novels of Gilmore Simms — paled in comparison. Why not enrich my offering by covering the whole range included in a new title I proposed to myself. "The *Cultural* History of Charleston, 1760 - 1860": artistic, intellectual, and scientific as well as *literary* history? In two of these areas I lacked expertise: but here I had at hand for art history excellent treatises based on primary sources, and for the history of science in the South, well, that was the specialty of a colleague at Duke. My reading and note-taking at the Library Society took on a new and expanded life, and the outlines and drafts scribbled off in my study on Elliott Street reflected a new enthusiasm.

3

Doors Opening:
Old Houses And New Friends

But enough of this food for thought. Time now for
another kind of sustenance: delightful experiences at
the hospitable tables of new friends in several of the
old houses in this quiet city, dedicated to privacy. With
visitors half a century ago Charleston had a reputation for being, shall we say, something less than New
York or Paris as a place for dining out. There was
Henry's, with authentic Charlestonian cuisine and
very good too, served with skillful courtesy by black
waiters, but that was the only restaurant to speak
of. There were other places where you could get ade-
quately fed, and there were the two hotels with what
could pass for "international" menus. This was all
that was available for visitors, except for the wealthy
few who might be guests at the elegant Villa Mar-
guerita, a late nineteenth-century colonnaded house
on South Battery transformed into a select residence-
hotel. Of course, the Carolina Yacht Club probably
set an even better table in those years before it had
tripled in size, but this was for members only. We did
not have the pleasure of sampling the fare at either
of these two centers of culinary art. Why this dearth

of dining-out places?

Back in 1938 there were not many tourists to cater to. And for natives the food at home and at the hospitable tables of friends was so special why should anyone be interested in dining out, except for an occasional dinner at Henry's? Although visitors, we were fortunate enough to experience this ourselves. The memorable luncheon at Miss Alice Smith's house was a foretaste of hospitality to come. Sam Stoney had apparently heard about our new friendships, and kindly extended our experiences by an invitation to Sunday dinner. He "borrowed" his mother's dining room (he lived in cozy bachelor's quarters in a wing at the back), and for this special treat he also "borrowed" the retired family butler, Faber, to cook the dinner. A venerable white-haired black man with an impressive presence, which had won him the honor he was proudest of, Carriage-Starter at the St. Cecilia Ball. He was also the most famous cook in Charleston, according to Sam, and this was the important thing for us. (Our invitation to the annual cotillion for debutantes didn't come until some years later.) Our dinner at the Stoney's Tradd Street home, centered on a succulent shrimp pilau, was superb in every way. So much so that Genie asked afterwards if she could deliver her compliments to the cook. In her visit to the kitchen she followed this with a request for his receipt. "Be glad to tell you Miss Eugenia," he said, "but won't do much good. First time I try a receipt I do it straight. Next time a little to the right, then a little to the left. Finally, it's Faber's own. But you got to know how to tease 'em along."

The next memorable event in our education as Charleston gourmets was the invitation to dinner at the "Pirate's House" on upper Church Street, home of Mrs. Goodwin Rhett, author of *Two Hundred Years of Charleston Cooking* (1930). Some local wit — was it Sam? — spoke of it as *Two Hundred Pounds of Charleston Cooking*, referring to how she had prospered from sampling her own receipts. The focal point of this really professional repast was a casserole of partridges, broiled over the open fire in her dining room, served with a special Madeira sauce. We bought her book the next day and it became our guide to the culinary secrets of this city for over a decade, until that classic of Southern cooking *Charleston Receipts* was published in 1950 by the Junior League, now well into the hundreds of thousands of copies sold. Goodwin Rhett was writing his reminiscences, and she asked me to read them and make suggestions for a publisher. Meanwhile Genie began profiting from Blanche Rhett's cook book. Although Lucile gave us good daily examples of local dishes, like all Charleston cooks she came in time for breakfast but left after our two o'clock dinner, so that we were on our own for the evening meal. Genie enjoyed trying her hand at light suppers, with her new book of receipts, making good use of the varied seafood and wide range of fruits and vegetables abounding in the market of this subtropical city by the sea.

4

The Fascination Of
Ante-Bellum Charleston

Cheered and strengthened with all this fine sustenance, I was prepared to return to my professional
regime of food-for-thought, digging and delving into
the past. During the century and a half that ended
with the Civil War, Charleston was the setting for
more historical dramas than any other city in America. Battles with Indians, Spaniards from Florida,
and pirates on the high seas; leading roles in the Revolutionary War and the founding of an independent
republic; the first to secede from that Union and to fire
on the flag, thus launching a catastrophic War
Between the States; not to mention recurrent fires
and hurricanes, plagues of Yellow Fever and Malaria,
a slave revolt and a devastating earthquake. Yet even
while coping with these tumultuous events Charleston
surpassed all the other Southern cities in amassing
wealth and in cultivating literature and the arts,
notably architecture. What made my researches in
the cultural life of ante-bellum Charleston so fascinating was the prospect of digging up these forgotten treasures to set against such a dramatic historical background.

The South Carolina Gazette (1732-1802) is the oldest continuous historical record of the state, especially of its famous city, and the Charleston Library Society had a complete file. Frail little Miss Ellen took particular pride in it, and insisted on fetching the huge bound volumes from the stacks by herself and plopping them down in front of me, one after another as the weeks went on. "It's all to be put on film, so copies can be placed in the great libraries," she said. "That's quite proper I know, as a librarian should, and we'll get in exchange films of rare files at the Worcester Antiquarian Society, and such. But it's really a shame," she added with the trace of a wink, "that those Yankee scholars won't have to come here to consult it in its proper ambience!" For my expanded topic, "A Cultural History of Charleston", I needed to cast a much wider net than just the volumes written by literary authors. I must comb the files of local newspapers, weeklies, monthlies, and quarterlies; take notes, then pursue my quarry. This meant a revision of my professional schedule. At the Library Society I would devote my time to journals of all sorts, reference works, compendiums, and other tomes either too heavy to take home or not allowed out on loan.

When I left for our two o'clock dinner, I'd take with me an armful of smaller volumes to read in the afternoons or evenings, depending on our personal schedule. If it was a heavenly afternoon we might devote it to a stroll or a historical-architectural prowl, guide books in hand, and defer our readings till after supper. If we were going out in the evening to dinner or the theater, the afternoon would be our reading session. Some of the books I borrowed from the library proved quite suitable for reading aloud together: William Elliott's *Carolina Sports by Land and Water* (1846), Elizabeth Allston Pringle's *A Woman Rice Planter* (1913), and Susan Petigru King's spicey novels about ante-bellum Charleston society. The volumes of heavier stuff, like Hugh Legare's essays on the classics, I studied alone with notebook in hand, while Genie entertained herself with some lighter social history. Our way of life in Charleston was settling into an ideal routine of labor and leisure, books and people, past and present.

Good literature should provide both pleasure and instruction, declared some eighteenth-century pundit (Dr. Johnson, perhaps?). The same was true of our walks in Charleston, which proved delightful as well as valuable aspects of our educational program. In these walks we combined our enjoyment of the present with our study of the past. Charleston was not only outstanding for its role in American history, but in the extraordinary number of its surviving architectural monuments. For us a special source of pleasure was Charleston's notable difference from other American cities we had known: older (founded in 1670), more complex, and above all richer in the quiet beauty of its buildings and its setting. Particularly striking was its contrast with the one we had just left, the town Duke University was incongruously situated on the edge of — Durham, North Carolina, a sprawling tobacco-factory town dating from the 1890's, its noisome prosperity such that it went on unabated through the Depression years! "Charleston is a civilized city in the European sense," a visitor from England remarked to us one day out of the blue. "It is a city to walk in, unique in your bustling country."

So we walked and walked for the sheer joy of it, sometimes adding a little history lesson to double the reward. On Tradd Street we stopped to admire the fine house once lived in by John Stuart, the Colonial Indian Commissioner, a lucrative post. In White Point Garden there was a marker where Stede Bonnet, the gentleman-pirate, was hanged in 1718. In the green oasis of Washington Park, behind the early 19th century City Hall, was the accidentally famous statue of William Pitt the Younger, erected in the 1760's by grateful Charlestonians to this British statesman who had almost single-handedly espoused their Cause in the pre-Revolutionary struggles over taxation-without-representation. Its "fame" dates from the bombardment of Charleston in 1780 when a shell from the British fleet struck off his arm. The one he had raised with an eloquent gesture during his famous speech in Parliament? Another prowl, which occupied several afternoons, was our search for the site of the "bastions" on the defensive wall built around the

lower city during the early decades to ward off threatened invasions from Spanish Florida, the rival colony
to the south. After the English buffer-colony of Georgia was established in the 1730's, these fortifications
were no longer needed so they fell into neglect. Our
explorations, unprofessional and casual in the
extreme, found no trace of them. But it was interesting to know that these old "bastions" had given the
names to South Battery and East Battery, two of the
loveliest waterfront walks in Charleston.

We had looked out at Fort Sumter from the Battery often, and one day we decided to take the excursion boat there across the harbor. Our history book
said that a Major Robert Anderson was the Yankee
commander forced to surrender when Sumter was
fired on at the outbreak of the Civil War. No kin, but
he happened to have the same name as my father.
Later, in a more detailed local history, I learned that
a Captain Clifford Anderson, leading a company of
the Macon Volunteers had come over from Georgia
in the middle of the war to help the Carolina Con-
federates defend Fort Johnson against the Yankee
army surging up from Beaufort. This one was a kins-
man, my grandfather to be exact. Yet somehow this
episode had dropped out of family reminiscences,
probably because this brief incident was eclipsed by
his earlier service on the battle front in Virginia and
his term in the Confederate Congress at Richmond
which followed. Anyhow, we made a picnic excursion

out to Fort Johnson and wandered around the ruins, looking back at Charleston and across the harbor to Sumter.

The architectural aspect of our peripatetic education was even more enjoyable than the historical, the visual mode being basic to art, as reading is basic to history. But we did our homework by reading the best guide books before taking our architectural tours. The Octagon Library volume *Charleston* (1927) by professional architects Albert Simons and Samuel Lapham, and Stoney's *Charleston: Azaleas and Old Brick* (1937) a volume in lighter vein, helped us to spot the special places and features to concentrate on. We learned about single- and double-houses Charleston style, the several kinds of bond used in brick work, noted the variety of orders on the capitals of the grander piazzas, sought out the choicest old gateways and balconies with Alston Deas' *Early Ironwork of Charleston* to guide us. But we were not all that serious as students of architecture. We were chiefly busy enjoying the beauty of these fine old Georgian houses with their unique Charlestonian touches. The beauty of the exterior quite naturally prompted a desire to see the interiors, but only two of the finest old houses were open to the public on a regular basis back then, the Heyward-Washington on Church Street and the Joseph Manigault on Meeting, the latter still in the process of being restored and so only sparsely furnished. We visited both on several occasions, and

Miles Brewton-Pringle House

(Watercolor by Paul Hogarth, R.A.)

longed for more. We were especially keen to see the interior of one that was not open to the public, the Nathaniel Russell House with its free-flying spiral stairway, pictured in one of our books, but it couldn't be arranged.

Meanwhile, one of our friends came up with something much better, an invitation to tea at the Miles Brewton-Pringle House, one of the truly great Georgian houses in America, to meet two elderly sisters, the Misses Sue and Mary Frost, now living in quiet retirement after an active life. So our pleasure was doubled: this stately home with its rich interior detail of craftsmanship, absorbed by us in the presence of these two remarkable ladies, who were an important part of old Charleston, especially in the active work of Miss Sue in saving some of the old houses on Tradd Street. Our endless walks through the old city and our privileged glimpses into some of its finest old houses, still lived in by descendants of the original owners, brought back to mind Henry James's account in *The American Scene* of his visit to Charleston three decades earlier, in 1905, romantic in tone though a bit tongue-in-cheek. The city kept reminding him of somewhere in Europe, with the faded glory of its old houses, the retreat of its gentry into the privacy of shuttered drawing-rooms, the air of peace that hung over its once active business area. All bespoke a heyday long past, reminiscent of some old Italian city. That was it: to James, Charleston seemed like the site of "some Venice that had never quite mustered!" The vistas of harbor and river on all sides and the canal-like network of waterways surrounding the city were the final touch that prompted his comparison to Venice, the fabled city-built-in-the-sea.

Our city walks continued throughout the year, purely for pleasure, though some of them did serve also to fill gaps in our education. Sometimes we had the advantage of Sam Stoney as our guide, a lively talker and a brisk walker, swinging his polished West Indian stick and using it to point out whatever was noteworthy. Sam could quite properly be described as an animated history book of Charleston. (Fortunately, some of that oral history found its way into print a few years later, when he wrote the text for *This is Charleston: A Survey of the Architectural Heritage*, published by the Carolina Art Association in 1944. It was based on Helen McCormick's reports and photos of 1,168 old houses, churches, and public buildings in Charleston worth preserving, ranged under five categories from Nationally Important to Worthy of Mention. This *Survey* provided the Preservation Society and the newly formed Historic Charleston Foundation with a goal they could direct their activities toward.)

Our walks with Sam Stoney made it clear that in old Charleston the devotion to beauty, with a flair for grandeur, extended to its splendid old churches and a surprising number of handsome public buildings that have survived from the early period. The Exchange Building, erected just before the Revolutionary War, makes an impressive eastern terminus to Broad Street. On either side of that are numerous banks and office buildings, as well as the City Hall, dating from the first years of the Republic. At the other end of Broad, on the Ashley River, stands the West Point Rice Mill, long idle and somewhat neglected back in 1938, but striking in the handsome brickwork of pilasters and pediment lavished on an ante-bellum mill. On Meeting Street just north of Broad, is a structure Charleston is particularly proud of, Robert Mills' landmark Fireproof Building completed in 1826, said to be the first such in America. This is a sampling of the buildings we admired from the outside, the interiors not being accessible back in 1938.

The churches were open to the public, of course, visitors as well as worshippers, and we spent pleasant hours in them and their adjacent churchyards. St. Michael's and St. Philip's first of all. Their soaring spires had served as landfalls for ships, the former with its bells, the latter with its beacon. The two oldest churches in Charleston (though St. Philip's had been rebuilt after a fire), they were notable as colonial examples of the Wren style. So we took our time enjoying the quiet elegance of their design, then lingered long in their tranquil churchyards, filled with memorials to the city's distinguished dead, including some of national fame: Draytons and Middletons, Pinckneys and Pringles and Rutledges.

Although the Episcopal church remained dominant, Charleston after the first decades had opted for religious toleration, and many denominations and sects added their fine buildings to the local scene. The Lutheran and Unitarian churches on Archdale Street had contributed much to the city's cultural as well as its spiritual life. The former was presided over for many years by the Rev. John Bachman, friend and patron of Audubon. The latter brought from Boston Mr. Samuel Gilman and his author-wife Caroline, both of whom played active roles in Charleston's literary and intellectual life. The Quaker Meeting House was gone, but its cemetery still survived on King Street. The imposing colonnaded Scots Presbyterian Church on lower Meeting and the fine synagogue on Hasell Street were two more of historical interest: one belonging to an offshoot of the Congregationalists, the first dissenting group to come to the city; the other being one of the oldest Jewish congregations in America, mostly Sephardic. Finally, of those that stand out in memory, the neo-Gothic Huguenot Church, which still held one service a year in French as ritual tribute to an earlier time. There is also an amusing legend that hung on from that same earlier time: since a large part of the congregation consisted of a group of Huguenot immigrants whose plantations were some miles up the Cooper River, the obliging pastor varied the time of the morning service to fit the tides, so his parishioners could come to church on the ebb and return home on the flood tide. So Sam Stoney told us. In this remarkable city even walks purely for pleasure always yielded extra dividends of history and art.

5

A Sampling of
Lowcountry Plantations

Although we had by no means exhausted the architectural treasures of old Charleston, our loyal little band of friends wanted us to see some of the old plantations too, and offered to pave the way. Except for two places nearby on the Ashley which we were saving until the camellia and azalea seasons because of their famous gardens, Hampton some fifty miles north of the city was the only plantation open to the public in those days. We made the two hour drive up the coast to have a look at that house where George Washington had spent the night on his way to Charleston in 1791, now in the process of being restored. Then our friends came to the rescue by arranging for us to see some of the plantations nearer to the city that were not open to the public. Dear old Mrs. Kershaw got permission for us to drive, under her banner, over the new Cooper River bridge to nearby Boone Hall, with its splendid avenue of live oaks and its intact "street" of brick cabins that had housed the slaves. She told us gaily of the balls and house parties she had enjoyed there as a young lady. From these reminiscences of our delightful sponsor we absorbed some authentic atmosphere of what old Boone Hall had been like. But the original plantation house had burned down years ago, replaced in the early 1930's not by a replica of itself but by a house looking enough like "Tara" to have been used for filming scenes from *Gone With The Wind* — a claim made by the present owners for the tourist trade, but hotly denied locally. (In ante-bellum Charleston the neo-classical style with its colonnaded portico was mostly reserved for public buildings and churches. Elsewhere in America it was widely used for houses, and has become the stereotype of the Southern Mansion, in the movies and in the popular imagination.)

Even little Miss Ellen FitzSimons played an unexpected role in our plantation education. As the weeks passed she had extended her relation of librarian-to-the-researcher by becoming our good friend also. We accepted with pleasure her invitation to tea in her "ugly house on an ugly little street," as she roguishly described her perfectly nice modern flat on Savage Street. We were a bit puzzled at first by the two terms "tea" and "about six-thirty," until we guessed that she was using "tea" in the old-fashioned sense of supper. She met us at the door with such eager hospitality she still had in her hands the two magazines she had been thumbing through. "The *Nation* and the *New Republic*," she said; "I'm such a conservative old lady I have to read the radical magazines to keep the balance straight." As she put them down on the parlor table she called our attention to a new novel, an advance copy for possible library purchase of Steinbeck's *Grapes of Wrath*. "Full of bad words but a good book, and it's going to be a sensation," she said. "I'm ordering it because our readers need jolting. I know you'll like it." Genie was captivated by this fascinating little creature whom she was now at last getting to know, embodiment of Old Charleston but with an inquiring mind open to the New.

During the course of a most enjoyable evening, with lively conversation and a savory collation, she regaled us with memories of childhood days at Mulberry Castle, after we admired the little watercolor of it on her parlor wall. Mulberry plantation dates from the beginning of the 18th Century (1714); "castle" refers to its four towers and other fortification features, serving to protect this outpost against possible Indian attacks, located as it was some thirty miles from the provincial capital. So the legend runs. If we would care to see it, she would make the arrangements. Mulberry had been sold to northerners a few years ago. But she knew the owners slightly, well enough to ask permission for us to view it, from the outside only. But even that was worthwhile, she said: "It's a fine old house in the Jacobean style, and the setting in woods and water, civilized by landscaping, is superb." Miss Ellen drove out with us one Sunday in late autumn, a memorable outing.

Anna Rutledge made her contribution to the cause

too. First she took us to call on the elderly Miss Charlie Drayton, so named by her father when he despaired of a son-and-heir to carry on his name. During a pleasant visit at her home on East Battery Anna casually hinted that we would enjoy seeing Drayton Hall. She was most cordial: "Do show them where to drive in, if the entrance isn't too overgrown, and then walk around as much as you like. The house is all locked up, and it would be too complicated to have it opened." Drayton Hall had not been lived in for years, only used by the family for Christmas parties, receptions during the debutante season, and such occasions. We made it our occasion for a picnic, with Anna and Kitty Ravenel to guide our innocent eye by pointing out the Palladian features of its imposing architecture, notably the two-storied portico. Afterwards we sat on the bank of the Ashley for our lunch.

Our chief architectural guide during that year in Charleston, of course, was Sam Stoney, both in his books and in person as he accompanied us around the city and to two plantations. Medway, the Stoney place, was built in 1686, shortly after the colony was founded. It had been sold quite recently to a couple from New Orleans, and the only thing needed was a telephone call to give the green light so that Sam could escort us out to one of the most interesting of the *Plantations of the Carolina Low Country*, ideally situated on one of the tributaries of the Cooper River. With his book in hand, opened to the photos and architect's drawings, he linked them to the details we were now viewing from all possible angles. The crow-stepped gables, the complex structure of wings and entrances added over the years to this oldest brick house in South Carolina, and the other special features that could be studied from the outside, to which we were as usual confined. At the end of our tour we sat on a bench at the waterside while Sam expanded freely on his printed narrative with many anecdotes, some historical and some merely amusing. On our way back to the city we stopped, with our usual picnic basket, to have lunch on the grounds of Goose Creek Church, the early 18th century parish church for the Barbadian planters. Sam had a long and loving account of it in his book, being one of the honorary vestrymen for the annual service held by the small preservation group that has kept this colonial gem in repair. This was enhanced now with many anecdotes from its turbulent history, no need for embroidery this time!

On a later occasion he took us to nearby Fenwick Hall on Johns Island, where the owner was a good friend of his. Here we were graciously invited in for tea, so we were able to admire the interior craftsmanship as well as the exterior architecture of this good example of a Georgian country house. After tea Sam took us on a little tour of the abandoned rice fields along the Stono River, explaining the use of dykes and sluice gates for flooding, and other aspects of rice culture. But this plantation visit must have been much later in the year, probably the end of April, because I remember Sam scraping handfuls of gnats from his beard.

"Quite a plague as summer comes on," I ventured.

"Don't mind 'em a bit," he replied. "When the gnats come, the tourists go."

Even fifty years ago there were enough tourists to annoy some natives, but only during the peak garden season from mid-February to mid-April.

What we had been seeing in our plantation walkabouts was supplemented by what we were reading. The volumes by Stoney, Lapham, and Simons for modern professional guidance in matters architectural and historical. Small books from the previous century as testimony that Charlestonians had always taken pleasure in the plantation side of their way of life: such as John B. Irving's *A Day on Cooper River* (1842) and Charles Fraser's "Sketch Book" with its miniature watercolors painted during visits to the country seats of his friends. In 1938 one had to get permission to examine the manuscript original of the latter at the Gibbes Gallery. (In 1940 the Carolina Art Association brought out a splendid edition of this beautiful little example of Fraser's art, with Introduction and Notes by Alice Smith — now out of print, alas.)

In this way our present pleasures gave new life to my researches into the past, even as the records I was digging up of Charleston's earlier history enhanced our enjoyment of the current scene. We were living in two worlds at once, the present and the past — something quite different from "livin' in the past," the romanticized slogan for tourists today. In ante-bellum times, despite transportation problems, Charleston and the Lowcountry had formed a single community, the same families moving in and out of the city with the seasons and with the changing priorities of their lives, very much as in England at the same period. This dual sense of place, merging rural and urban, survived at least in feeling right on down to the late 1930's, the world we came to know and cherish.

6

Sharing The Wealth

Although we had explored only a small sample of old Charleston's town and country houses, we now felt sufficiently qualified to serve as amateur guides for visitors from outside the state. So began our invitations to family and friends with whom we wanted to share the wealth. Our first guest was Sarah Wadley Burt, a very special friend of ours though she was almost my mother's age. We knew we would enjoy her and had every reason to believe she'd enjoy Charleston. Shortly after World War I, Sarah had inherited the Wadley plantation and had been struggling heroically ever since to rescue it from years of neglect. By leasing most of the fields to neighboring farmers and concentrating her efforts on a dairy, which was prospering, she had managed to restore the house, bring back the century-old boxwood garden, and otherwise tidy up the acres immediately around Great Hill Place. Since it was just about an hour's drive from my native town of Macon, Georgia, when home on holidays we would often go out for a visit. We might find her in her book-lined library reading Jane Austen, one of her favorite volumes of early Georgia history, a book on Italian art, whatever the mood called for. Or she might have to be summoned from the barnyard by ringing the plantation bell. In which case, when she appeared in boots and with her long hair tumbling onto her shoulders, she would put it back deftly with a couple of hairpins, slip into a pair of French highheels on the back porch, and presto! the dairy farmer transformed into the lady! "The mint patch is over there, you remember. I'll fetch the Bourbon and the ice, and we'll meet under the magnolias for a julep." As she strode across the lawn, accompanied by her two Irish setters, I sometimes found myself wondering if she might have some Indian blood in her veins — that long black hair, dark brown almost black eyes, and boldly chiselled features. After all, this had been Cherokee country! As we sat under the magnolia trees there would be much laughter, civilized conversation, some talk about Great Hill Place and its most recent improvements, if we prodded her.

When Sarah arrived in Charleston early in December, driven over by her journalist son George who hoped to write a few travel pieces for the *Macon Telegraph*, we learned about her newest plans. They added two specific reasons why she was eager to visit this old city. She wanted to study the different kinds of brick walls here, because she was planning to build a long wall at Great Hill Place to separate her spruced up back yard from the unavoidable mess of the dairy — cow shed, milking barn, the whole lot. Over the next few days she was especially taken with two types of brick walls in Charleston: one with recessed panels between the thicker pillars, another with open-work panels between. Both of these styles enable you to build a much longer wall with the same quantity of bricks. And Sarah wanted to build several hundred feet of wall with her limited supply of lovely old bricks from a collapsed outbuilding. Her other new plan was to extend her garden from the boxwood labyrinth down into the woods, with azaleas and camellias. This project high-lighted our trip out to Middleton Place, the ideal Lowcountry plantation to take her to for several reasons.

The focus of attention at Middleton is on the garden rather than the house, only one wing having survived the raiders from General Sherman's army. Great Hill Place, being directly in the path of Sherman's March through Georgia, had been laid waste though the simple plantation house had been miraculously spared. At Medway and Mulberry these grand houses are the center of interest rather than their surrounds. But in the first place they were not available to us for a second visit. Besides, they had been restored to perfection by waving the wand of outside wealth, a consummation devoutly to be thankful for. But such magical transformations might overwhelm Sarah's will to carry on her endless struggle. What was going on at Middleton Place, still in the original family, struck a more kindred note, though on a scale that made it quite beyond comparison with such modest places as Sarah's. The present owner, Mr. Pringle Smith, was also struggling heroically to restore his inherited plantation after some years of neglect. First, to bring the formal gardens back to their original splendor as laid out in the 1740's, the first landscaped garden in America. Then to extend the newer woodland areas of camellias and azaleas. In the 1930's Middleton Place was being opened to the public on certain days for a fee, to help defray these expenses. It was there we took the Burts, mother and son, for a wonderful day in December. The Camellia Sasanquas were in full bloom, to Sarah's delight, the later flowering Japonicas only in bud. As we wandered over to the azalea hillside beyond the mill pond, George managed to extract a few choice bits of Middleton Place history from Pringle Smith, who was supervising the new plantings there, while Sarah asked one of the garden staff some questions about azaleas. So few tourists in those days we were treated like guests!

Only a part of this all too short visit was spent solving Sarah's problems for her home place. We found time for long walks around the city, while George presented his credentials at the *News and Courier*, even achieving a brief interview with the famous and rather crotchety editor W. W. Ball. Sarah took pleasure in strolling through the old market, and lingering along the water front, a great treat for one from the Piedmont of Georgia. There were some of our Charleston friends to meet, and some Charleston dishes to try, Sarah having a responsive palate. By good luck Sheridan's *School for Scandal* was on at the Dock Street, and this racy Restoration comedy gave us a happy theater evening. On the last night before their departure from No. 5 Elliott Street, Sarah impulsively took a large topaz pendant from round her neck and hung it on Genie's. "My father bought it for me in Florence, on my eighteenth birthday trip to Europe. Now I'm a country woman and seldom go out, or even dress up. You wear it. It goes well with your earrings." What a guest!

My parents, Gertrude and Robert Lanier Anderson, were our next guests, driving over from Macon at the end of January. Their special interests in visiting Charleston were quite different from Sarah Burt's, of course, so our plans for them brought into play different aspects of this many-faceted old city and promised to be entertaining for us too. Gert was more interested in people than places, cared more about the art-of-living (as she termed it) than about any of the fine arts, and had her own definition of the acceptable "old": traditional was fine, but nothing musty or fusty. Robbie had some special interests also, but was too much of a gallant knight to his lady to obtrude them. So he went along genially with whatever she wanted, biding his turn.

First of all we paid a call on dear Margaret Kershaw, so the two ladies could feast on memories of old times in Macon when they were neighbors, just across a little park. The good Dr. Rutledge had now recovered and my father found much to talk about with him, both being professional men and old fashioned in their tastes. Meanwhile, Gertrude was deeply involved learning about old furniture from Anna's mother. She had been obsessed with "antiques" ever since the early 1920's when her husband inherited the Anderson home, a comfortable but undistinguished mid-Victorian house. She had joyfully supervised its restoration, to get rid of the shabbiness that had overtaken it during the quarter-century of grandmother's widowhood, when Judge Anderson's death severed her last link with the Old South. Gertrude's "improvements" included modernization of kitchen and bathrooms, naturally, but they also involved a bit of "face-lifting" I'm afraid. She wanted to keep everything traditional, she maintained, but she wanted her home full of light and air.

Mrs. Kershaw's 18th century house seemed a bit too dim and shuttered to Gertrude. No. 44 South Battery, only a decade or so older than her own home, was much more to her liking. Light and airy also and (by reason of its ampler and finer architectural design) with no need of face-lifting. After restoring the Anderson home, Gert's next passion had been to sweep it clean of its over-stuffed late Victorian furniture and to scour Macon for the kind of antiques that had been discarded by grandmother, recovering when possible family pieces stored in attic and cellar or given to faithful retainers. In a comparatively new city like Macon, not founded until the 1820's, "antiques" meant Empire at the earliest. In Charleston, she was discovering, the best furniture came from an earlier period: Chippendale, Hepplewhite, Sheraton. An exciting new chapter in her education was opening up.

Some of our friends were invited to Elliott Street for drinks or dinner to meet our family. The big hit was Sam Stoney, as expected. Gert was quite taken with his combination of gallantry and deviltry, a brand new experience. His genealogical tales, lacing the annals of distinguished families with spicey anecdotes, had her on the edge of her seat. Afterwards she told me she was not shocked, but added that some of his stories certainly were risqué and "he sure does cuss a lot." I had heard nothing more than a peppering of damn-damn-damn, and a few salty allusions to long ago *affaires*. Robbie was more interested in Sam's serious accounts of Charleston history, which poured out now that he had new ears to welcome them. On the lighter side, his famous Gullah sermon on the creation of Adam and Eve in the Garden of Eden had all of us rolling. Genie, with her stage experience, knew just when to work in a cue that would bring our actor to the footlights.

It was Sam who also alerted us to the concert being staged in classical Hibernian Hall by the Society for the Preservation of Spirituals. This was performed entirely by whites, but it was no Blackface Minstrel Show. They were ladies and gentlemen, descendants of the rice-planting gentry, who sang the majestic tunes and moving words as they remembered hearing them sung by blacks in the Lowcountry, with clapping hands and occasional dance steps. They were all in ante-bellum costumes, I must add, but these were heirlooms. Everything dignified and authentic.

Gertrude's preference for people over places? In Charleston the two sometimes merged. History and art also merged in our strolls round the old city, both parents being good walkers. We gave them a tour of the Heyward-Washington House so they'd have one example of the city's finest architecture and furnishings. But what with invitations to our friends' houses, there was no need to press on them a more serious study of Charleston's artistic heritage. For history, I told my father about the battle of Fort Sumter with Yankee Major Anderson, a non-kinsman, defending; and the battle of Fort Johnson with Captain Clifford Anderson, his father, coming with the Macon Volunteers to join the defending Charleston troops. Both interested him so much that we made excursions anew to both places.

What appealed to Robbie most of all were Charleston's old churches. Being the ruling elder of the First Presbyterian Church of Macon, with ancestors from Scotland in two main branches of his family, he naturally chose the service at the old Scots Presbyterian Church for his first Sunday. When their visit was extended to include a second Sunday, I primed him for the service at St. Michael's by showing him a delightful little Confirmation Book by one of the first South Carolina bishops, printed in the early 1790's shortly after America's break with the Anglican hierarchy. In his preface the Charleston bishop had said: "Remember, young people, that God is a gentleman and expects good manners in all things" — or words to that effect. Robbie had a more serious reason in opting for St. Michael's, citing the fact that his great grandfather had been an Episcopal rector in Virginia, and that his legal vocation and religious avocation made him especially partial to a church located on one of the "Four Corners of Law." On a walking tour we had pointed out the four buildings at the intersection of Broad and Meeting Streets that made this place so revered by Charlestonians: the City Hall dating from 1801, the County Courthouse from the end of the 18th century, the late 19th century federal building housing both Post Office and U.S. courts (described by Kitty Ravenel as "pork-barrel Victorian"), and St. Michael's built in 1751, symbolizing the law of God.

One after another, Charleston was able to fulfill all my parents' special interests. One of Gertrude's I've failed to mention so far. She was an ardent gardener, though limited in range because she did not come into a place of her own until past middle age and even then it was only a city lot. Remembering her love of the spectacular, we decided on Magnolia rather than Middleton for a sample of the great plantation gardens. Here she could swoon over the massed camellias now in full bloom; the brilliant banks of azaleas, doubling themselves with reflections in the water (she had the true gardener's imagination that can anticipate flowering seasons); occasional tall pines with cascades of wisteria and Lady Banksia roses, already showing their lavender and gold blossoms; the stately magnolia grandiflora that would fill the woods later on with the glory that had astonished early explorers like the Bartrams. This was our show piece. Back in the city there were modest treats, nearer to the size of her small garden in Macon which had prospered under her dedicated care. In Charleston she could catch many gratifying glimpses of long established urban gardens, because in those halcyon pre-tourist days if a gate was left ajar this meant that visitors were welcome to come in and peek around.

Our final garden treat came as a surprise to us all. On the morning when my parents were attending service at St. Michael's, Genie and I were leafing lazily through the Sunday papers when we stumbled on our discovery. Cypress Gardens would be open to the public this weekend for the first time this year. A most imaginative and enterprising couple, husband from New York and wife a Charlestonian, had transformed an old rice plantation reservoir into a water-garden.

After an early lunch the four of us set off on the hour long drive up the coast to see this new creation.

During the decades of dereliction the reservoir had reverted to swamp. The unique way of seeing this garden is in flatbottom boats, with a skilled black oarsman to guide you safely through the labyrinth of "Bald Cypress" trees whose trunks rise up toward heaven but "breathe through their knees" in the water, which is turned inky black by the tannin in their bark. The perfect mirror reflection in the water of tree tops and sky creates the illusion that you are floating in a magical world. The old dykes are planted thick with jonquils and daffodils now all a-blaze, azaleas to flower later in this all but sunless place, festoons of wild jasmine already lighting their candles and perfuming the air in the first swamp-garden we'd ever seen. The climax for Gertrude came when we docked at the end of our cruise and walked down a long embankment of *daphne odora*, its creamy-pink flowers diffusing the most concentrated fragrance she had ever inhaled. "I must have some for my Georgia garden!" A consultation with the caretaker, the address of a nursery for purchases, and we drove back to Charleston with an elated mother and contented father.

The timing of their visit was auspicious in another way, though one not really relevant to Charleston except in the sense of opposites being complementary. It so happened that February 1 was the publication date of my first book, *Melville in the South Seas.* (The discovery of a cache of Melville MSS had turned me to that subject, replacing the biography of Charleston poet Paul Hayne, the original subject of my Ph. D. thesis.) In 1841 that adventurous young gentleman Herman Melville had shipped on a whaling vessel bound to the Pacific, a voyage that led to the discovery of a primitive Paradise in the South Sea Islands, the relation of fact to fiction in Melville's novels being the subject of my researches. Now, nearly a century later I was exploring the relationship of history to legend in the civilized paradise of ante-bellum Charleston, South Carolina!

By way of celebration my parents had brought with them as a gift from Eugenia's Auntie, at whose house we had been married, a Charleston rice spoon engraved: "To Honor Herman Melville's Debut" — a silver symbol linking the two explorations of paradise, worlds apart! The Charleston Rice Spoon has been immortalized by Sam Stoney: "Of massive silver, about fifteen inches long and broad in proportions, it is laid on the cloth of every proper Charleston dinner table with something of the reverential distinction that surrounds the mace in the House of Commons at Westminster. And their functions are not dissimilar, for if you take away the bauble, as did Cromwell, the Commons of England are a mob without authority, and if you take away the rice-spoon from the Charleston dinner table, the meal that follows is not

really dinner." (*Charleston: Azaleas and Old Brick*).
With our new silver symbol we could sit down to
authentic Charleston dinners.

By way of thanks to Aunt Dolly, we sent her an
autographed copy of my book, and gave one to my
parents. Melville's novels were not exactly Robbie's
dish, but he was proud of having an author-son, to
keep up a family tradition, as he reminded me. His
father had codified the laws of Georgia; his great-
uncle Joseph LeConte was the author of numerous
scientific books, including one trying to reconcile evo-
lution and religion, and ending his career with a
highly readable autobiography; his cousin Sidney
Lanier had won a small measure of fame in the 19th
century with his volumes of poetry and his essays on
The Science of English Verse. So on this bookish note
Rob and Gertrude's visit to Charleston came to a sat-
isfying conclusion.

7

Research Into The Past

But what of my second book? A sabbatical year, no less than good literature in Dr. Johnson's definition, should combine learning and pleasure. But from the trend of life in Charleston during recent weeks my research at the Library Society was in danger of being lost in a welter of enjoyment. To revive my enthusiasm for the cultural history of Charleston I began work on an essay I had promised to contribute to a volume now being prepared "In Honor of Kenneth Boyd," the distinguished professor of Southern History at Duke and founder of our Americana Club at that university. The cue for my topic was a series of articles I had been reading on "Ante-bellum Charleston", published in the *Southern Bivouac* by Paul Hayne in the 1880's. These I planned to compare with the reminiscences in a long sequence of letters exchanged during the same period between the poet Hayne and a Creole historian in New Orleans named Charles Gayarré. The MSS were part of a large collection I had helped bring to Duke when I joined the faculty in 1931. Now a trip there enabled me to borrow these letters from the archives and bring them to my

Charleston study, where I could weave them into my essay for the Boyd volume. As the two old boys got going in their private reminiscences of the "good old days before the war," they opened the floodgates of nostalgia with no thought of restraint. But when Hayne prepared his articles on the same ante-bellum period for a magazine, the discipline required for publication brought the proper controls. The contrast between these two modes of dealing with sentimental memories was the theme of my essay entitled "Gayarré and Hayne: the Last Literary Cavaliers," a narrative that ran to sixty pages.

The hazards posed by indulgence in nostalgia are made memorable by Oscar Wilde, that master of the bon mot, in his anecdote of a visit to Charleston in 1883 (the date of the Hayne-Gayarré correspondence). He had never imagined what ruin war could bring, we are told, until one night on the High Battery looking out to Fort Sumter he turned to some one and said, "How beautiful the moon is!" only to get for a reply, "You should have seen it, sir, before the War!" I made a mental note of this to guide me in writing my own reminiscences.

My work on the cultural history of Charleston, stimulated by writing the essay on Hayne and Gayarré, was now back in full swing. Our routine returned to the happy combination of learning about the past and enjoying the present in Charleston, the schedule with which our sabbatical year had begun.

The stream of guests from out of town was over for the present, so more time was available for rewarding research at the Library and pleasurable reading at No. 5 Elliott Street. The cultural heritage of this city was unfolding with a richness and variety beyond my expectations, and the number of books on ante-bellum Charleston we found entertaining enough for reading aloud together was quite surprising.

Eagerly at work though I was researching the past, we were both still alert to present pleasures, especially in the evenings. In addition to more plays at the Dock Street Theater and an occasional lecture on art, there was one musical event of unique distinction. A group of black people from Edisto, actually a whole congregation from a church on that island in the heart of Gullah country, came up to Charleston in a farm truck and put on a performance to raise money for repairing their roof. Where it was staged slips my memory — in an old movie house? a small auditorium? — but what happened on stage was unforgettable. It was not a show, but a regular church service enacted unselfconsciously just as it would have occurred on any Sunday in their own church building. The stage props were quite simple: a lectern to serve as pulpit, rows of chairs for pews, a roped off place for the choir. Costumes: simply their "Sunday best." The preacher gave an eloquent sermon, rousing enough to raise that roof, calling on the brothers and sisters to dig deep in their pockets for the collection plate. "Thought religion was free!" a voice cried from the back pew. "So it is, like water," the parson replied, "but costs money to pipe it to you."

To coax the contributions along, from audience rather than performers, the singing started. As it got under way, material concerns yielded to spiritual, and the "shouting" began. This is an Americanization of the African word *saut*, that has nothing to do with raising your voice in a shout. It's the term for a "ring dance," a New World survival of the song-dance ritual for pagan ceremonies in West Africa, adapted by slaves in America for the Christian religion, to which they were converted belatedly in the 19th century. The singing started with ante-bellum slave hymns, moved on to post-war spirituals, then began to slide into 20th century blues. At this point some of the younger women began to sway their hips. "Lift them feet, sister!" the preacher warned. We had never heard anything like it! Except once, an equal spiritual fervor but for an entirely different occasion. Our next door neighbors on Elliott Street, a dignified black family, were stricken with the death of a loved one. The kin from all round came and sat up with the body throughout the night, alternately moaning and wailing: the grand old spirituals, "Oh, sometimes it causes me to tremble," followed by the unsuppressed lamentation, "And did they crucify my Lord!"

Here surely was an extraordinary manifestation of Charleston's cultural heritage, especially true of the Edisto church service: an Afro-American folk art combining song, dance, and a dramatic preacher/narrator to give it structure. A new kind of "opera"? or more properly "oratorio"? Eugenia, with her love of theater, of dance and music, was captivated. Over the years, her re-enactment of snatches from this performance, to entertain our friends, has kept my memory of it vivid. If I were writing about the 20th century I could claim it as a source for Dubose Heyward's *Porgy*, which had been transformed into a folk opera by inspired collaboration with George Gershwin. Although now hailed as a classic, *Porgy and Bess* is not only a hybrid of Harlem grafted on Charleston stock, but is a creation by Whites of a Black musical drama. How could I track down the ante-bellum forerunners of the "Edisto Oratorio" — Black art created by Blacks — in order to incorporate in my book this aspect of old Charleston's culture? A century ago there were no written records of such performances except by White observers, usually visitors from England, who only half understood what they were witnessing. It would take a great deal of research by trained cultural anthropologists to recapture what I wanted to find.

(In recent years this expectation has flowered in two splendid volumes: Lawrence Levine's *Black Culture and Black Consciousness* (1977) and Charles Joyner's *Down by the Riverside* (1984). The latter is a vivid recreation of the religious, musical, and general cultural life of slaves on the famous rice plantations of the Waccamaw up the Carolina coast, including a convincing new theory of the Gullah language: not a debased form of English by illiterate slaves, but a true Creole language based on West African syntax and grammatical forms adapted to an English vocabulary.)

Reluctantly I concluded that this was beyond my skills. Just as the important field of political writings and the whole military build-up to the disastrous Civil War were beyond the scope of my cultural history. Besides, such controversial topics as these would inevitably bring up the Slavery issues — Nullification, Abolition, Secession — that would engulf my story. Best to leave that Nemesis alone, brooding over the whole scene.

8

Living In The Present

As spring came on, the one real threat to steady work on book number two was the temptation to sit in the garden, our miniature paradise. This problem was solved by Genie's ingenuity in bringing the garden into the house. She kept it filled with flowers, partly our own and partly from an unexpected source. A new kind of street vendor had appeared at our gate one morning with the cry, "Got a flower gyarden on me haid!" And there was a tall mahogany-colored woman with a great circular basket brimming with color balanced on her head. One had read in the Old Testament and seen depicted on Greek vases the stately posture of women bearing water jugs and the like on their heads. Here it was, a *tableau vivant*! She came over several times a week from Mt. Pleasant on the ferry, which docked on East Bay not far above our street, and brought her welcome wares right to our doorstep. Another extra dividend.

Genie's little circle of friends filled her days with contentment, so I was free to drive ahead seriously with my research. I could always take time off for a half-hour bike ride before breakfast, of course, or longer still for a stroll at sundown. But occasionally the weather was so divine she called on me to strike my tasks and join her for a full day's outing, especially if it was on a weekend. One that stands out in memory was a long bicycle ride out to St. Andrews, the parish church for planters along the Ashley River in the old days. After we crossed the Ashley bridge, the old river road was a peaceful avenue of over-arching oaks draped with moss the whole way to St. Andrews and on beyond. Past Drayton, Middleton, Magnolia, and the other plantations, whose people had been the parishioners of this lovely little church nestled in a grove of trees.

It was a very warm day in May when we pedalled out to St. Andrews, and Genie's surprise package was an iced salad and a thermos of iced tea hidden away at the bottom of her bike basket, to accompany the devilled crabs and strawberries she had entrusted to my care. As we spread our picnic on a carpet of pine needles, our bikes tethered to a tree, we pictured to ourselves the planters' families of ante-bellum days, their carriages and horses cared for by servants, feasting on their more sumptuous dinners during the long midday break between Morning Prayers and Evensong, before returning to their respective homes. Our excursion had been purely for pleasure, yet I was able to turn it to account for my history also, because the social and religious aspects of plantation life played an interesting part in the writings of several Carolina ladies during the *ancien regime:* the novels of Susan Petigru King, the fictionalized memoirs of Mary Chestnut, and the "Recollections" of Caroline Gilman. Absorbing the scene at St. Andrews enabled me to visualize what a plantation Sunday there had been like a century ago. Imagination is a useful adjunct to documented facts in creating a readable historical narrative.

With such an ideal pattern for our lives, the weeks slipped into months, and our year was drawing to a close before we realized it. Just how blissfully we had been floating along in a dream world was revealed when our bank statement of June 1 arrived. The entire amount of my Rosenwald grant had already been paid to us, and spent, in nine monthly installments covering the "academic year." This meant that we would have nothing but my half salary from Duke to cover all expenses during the remaining three months of our full "sabbatical year." A crisis calling for a summit! We sent an S. O. S. to Sam Stoney, our constant adviser. After dinner we told him of our plight. We had hoped to extend the lease on Elliott Street, but $85 a month was more than we could spare from our remaining pittance. Sam had an idea. "My house down on Folly Beach I count on to bring in my salad money in the summers. But this damn Depression hangs on, and no takers this year so far," he said. "Maybe you?" We jumped at the idea, and asked how much. "How much you got?" We told him $150 a month total.

"Lemme have $50 and you live on $100." Agreed. "Then Folly's yours for three months — provided I can come to dinner when I want to." We were ready to sign then and there, but he laughed, "Better see it first."

Next day we drove down the fifteen miles to Folly Beach, over the Ashley River, then south through James Island. After we crossed Wappoo Cut (the Inland Waterway) houses began to dwindle away, and for the most part our road was through sparsely settled country, with vistas of marsh land on one side of the road and groves of live oaks on the other. During the last few miles we passed occasional small docks for shrimp or fishing boats on the little creeks, wholesalers who supplied the Charleston markets, but with stands where we could buy, cheap. Also occasional stalls set up by small scale black farmers. "Get your fruits and vegetables there, better than in town," Sam pointed out. Over the last bridge, high enough for small sailing craft to pass beneath, and we were on Folly Island. As memory records, there were no hotels or restaurants on the island in those days. A Post Office with a small store for staples, a rustic pavilion for picnickers, and sandy roads leading off on left and right to little groups of houses nestled in clumps of trees right along the beach, the settled areas being few and far between.

Sam Stoney's house, our summer home in 1939, was typical of the beach houses on Folly in those days.

It was situated in a grove of live oaks and palmettos about a mile from the Post Office. Ample in size and simple in architecture: several bedrooms, on either side of a hall for sea-breezes, a combination living/dining room, adequate kitchen, and a bathroom with all facilities, which he proudly showed us: "Put in to attract paying guests like you." The whole structure was up on stilts as a precaution against flood tides and hurricanes. But part of this "ground floor" was boxed in to form a couple of extra bedrooms, a toilet, and an outside shower for swimmers to wash off the sand and salt. Elemental rather than really primitive, but it all seemed quite satisfactory to us.

We sat on the wide screened porch at the front, looking out through the trees to the ocean, and had a leisurely talk. "This is the best place for breakfast and dinner, except when it rains or blows hard," Sam said. "Inside's cooler at midday." Really good swimming here, he assured us, never crowded or noisy. Better than on Sullivan's (though old Charlestonians prefer it as "*the* Island"), where the beach is steeply shelving, with a dangerous undertow, and cut into little coves by erosion. "Here there are long stretches of smooth beach, so gently shelving it was used in early times to 'folly' small vessels, that is to 'beach' them for scraping barnacles and repainting. That's the meaning of Folly Beach."

This triggered the Great Raconteur, and several more anecdotes of island lore followed, some convincing, all entertaining. "Keep a few surfboards under here," he indicated; "good rollers coming in at high tide most days. I come down to swim and surf all through the year, except for winter months." Pointing to a couple of houses not far from his, he added that we'd have a few friends here. Tommy and Rowena Tobias owned one of them and the other would be used this summer by the Whitelaws. (It belonged to Dubose Heyward, who was not well at the moment. He died the next year, 1940.) The bargain was now struck and our simple contract signed, but with one proviso: "You must promise to come to dinner often, maybe once a week." Agreed. "Forgot to say there's no telephone," Sam said. "Hope you don't mind. There's a phone at the P.O. for emergencies, and you can get your newspapers there." We were delighted, and decided to skip the papers also. A real hide-away. Sam's visits would bring us news enough.

When we told our plans to Lucile, she accepted at once our invitation to go with us and "live in" for the three months. The next day we took her to Folly to have a look. Her private quarters on the ground floor pleased her, and when we said she could have our portable radio down there all to herself, she beamed. (Step by step we were making our retreat complete from the turbulent, disturbing world news of 1939.) Lucile checked out the kitchen equipment and made a short list of things needed. Back in town we went shopping for these items, and for several others to make our island life comfortable: two canvas lounge chairs and several campstools, a beach umbrella to stick in the sand, and two large beach towels. All these extras, and everything from Elliott Street not needed for daily living, we took down to Sam's house in advance of the hegira. There were a few days left before our lease ran out, and we made the best of them. I put in as many hours as possible at the Library Society to wind up the research that could only be done there. Last of all, I made out long lists of books I would be wanting to borrow on my weekly trips into the city. Miss Ellen FitzSimons connived, helpfully digging out a special rule that would allow an accredited research scholar to take out more books at a time than the usual allowance.

9

An Island Paradise – With Books

When mid June came we packed the car with all the rest of our possessions, including a lovely load of books, and made the great migration — from a long and happy life in Old Charleston to our anticipated summer idyll on Folly Beach. It took the better part of the afternoon to settle in. Then, while I organized one corner of the living room as my study, Genie took Lucile on a little walk-about, having arranged for her to meet the servants at the houses of our neighboring friends.

After an early supper, what better than to spend the first evening sampling the peace and quiet of our new island home. In our lounge chairs on the beach we lay back relaxed, just in time for that witching hour between twilight and the closing in of darkness. Watching the ebbing tide, listening to the sound of wind and wave and the last faint cries of seagulls, we were lapped in the peace of nature and the quiet music of the sea at night. Only poets can capture the song of the sea in all its infinite variety. Not presuming to enter that competition, I settled for quoting the finest lines I could remember:

Charm'd magic casements, opening on the foam
Of perilous seas, in fairy lands forlorn.

Thou who didst waken from his summer dreams
The blue Mediterranean, where he lay,
Lulled by the coil of his crystalline streams ...

There is a tide in the affairs of men,
Which taken at the flood, leads on to fortune; ...
On such a full sea are we now afloat.

These lines set in motion a train of thought, and
before I knew it I was thinking out loud. "It would be
interesting to see what those old Charleston poets
had to say about the sea — Hayne, Timrod, and the
others. Not up to Keats, Shelley, and Shakespeare,
to be sure. But they were surrounded by the sea on all
sides, so it must have been a recurrent subject. After
all, there are some sensitive lyrics in Josephine Pinckney's slender volume of *Sea-Drinking Cities*. Why not
the ante-bellum poets too?" Poetry was not Genie's
main line, but a project never failed to stir her. Rashly,
she undertook to read or at least to scan all those
hundreds of pages of verse turned out by Charlestonians between 1760 and 1860, and copy down the
lines dealing with the sea. A most valued research
assistant! I could make good use of such a topical
treatment of these poets — and other topics too, such
as landscapes, eulogies of country life, heroic episodes
of Carolina history — and so avoid treating minor

poetry by the stricter standards applied to poems that are created works of art.

And so to bed. Next day we began our new life, not on a desert island in the South Seas, but a wooded island paradise on the coast of South Carolina. The real paradox about Paradise is that every day is perfect but every day must be exactly like every other day. The best comment on this dilemma is the dream that an old lady had: God appeared in a cloud and said to her, "You have led such a good life, I hereby promise you eternal bliss." In the morning at breakfast the dream came back to her, and the maid heard her mumble, "I'm not sure I would care about just *that.*" We agreed with the old lady. Such a life style is cherished only by the idle rich. There is no possibility of our ever being rich, much less any desire to be so. And active involvement with living in all its possibilities is the center of our being. Let me start over. Next day we began a new phase of our old life which had given us so much joy during the last nine months. Not really a hide-away, as our Charleston friends had said they would pop in occasionally. Even so, the important thing was that we were now free to devote more time to the fascinating world of ante-bellum Charleston, the topic for my proposed book. The summer at Folly Island would not really be a retreat. We were still deeply engaged, though engaged in interpreting the past for those in the present who care about continuity and tradition.

First step was to set up our routine, keeping to our former pattern of work and play, study and relaxation, learning and enjoyment in proper proportions. For the three summer months emphasis would be placed on the first of these pairs. Because of the urgency of winding up my basic research before leaving the Charleston area, and the limited temptations to idle pleasures available at Folly Beach, this was only natural. Although the pleasurable side of our island life was to be subordinate, it was important to us nonetheless.

The first morning we got up an hour before breakfast, not for a bike ride but to take a swim. Rather, to help Genie to learn how to swim, then after that .... I began by slowly convincing her of the helpful buoyancy of salt water. Her previous dips had all been in fresh water pools, splashing and paddling in the shallow end, fearful of going to the bottom in deeper water. Now at the beach we waded out waist deep, and supporting her lying on her left side, I showed her the arm and leg motions of the side-stroke. Gradually I relaxed my support a bit so she could see how little effort was needed to keep afloat. Progress was slow, as all who've learned to swim know. After we practiced about half an hour, Genie sat on the beach and watched me demonstrate the side-stroke, average swimmer though I was. Last evening I had picked out a prominent stump at water line, a quarter-mile down coast from our house. That was to be her target, and such was her progress that she mastered this quarter-mile before the summer was over. The peaceful sounds of wind and wave that had soothed us last night were augmented during our morning swims by the chorus of mocking-birds, fluting of the wood thrush, and an occasional cardinal's song from a tree top staking out his territorial rights. Except for the birds, we had the beach all to ourselves at this early hour.

Refreshed by our swim, we stripped off under the shower, washing away sand and salt, then wrapped in our beach towels dashed upstairs to dress for breakfast. The mornings, when we felt most invigorated, were dedicated to the most exacting work. Genie kept to her promise of working her way heroically through all those pages of old Charleston poetry looking for passages inspired by the sea. I turned my attention first to all the volumes of miscellaneous prose outside the usual literary categories of poetry-fiction-drama. These continued to flourish in Charleston right down to my terminal date of 1860, much as they had in 17th and 18th century England. (Everything in ante-bellum Charleston seemed to be old-fashioned, even while it was happening!) To suit my expanded topic, the *Cultural* History of Charleston, I cast a wider and wider net.

When I decided to include the books and articles written by scientists, I found that I must extend "Charleston" to include Beaufort and Georgetown on the coast and up-state to Columbia. In a word the city and state were one. Scientific writing was an area of prolific intellectual activity in South Carolina throughout my chosen period. Some of the authors were doctors who preferred research to practice; some were planters, whose close connections with the natural world prompted scientific interests in several directions. A brief sampling will indicate something of their scope. And though the books cited deal with regional phenomena, their authors received national recognition as scientists for their work. Thomas Walter, *Flora Caroliniana* (1788); Stephen Elliott's two volume *Sketch of the Botany of South Carolina and Georgia* (1811, 1824); John Holbrook, *Ichthyology of South Carolina* (1855). The more popular works of two outside scientists form a kind of frame to the above: William Bartram's *Travels Through the Carolinas* (1791) and Audubon's *Birds of America* (1838).

Although I had decided not to include political writings, for fear of drowning my cultural narrative in the great controversy over slavery, that was easier said than done. For it turned out that in South Carolina as in the rest of America especially during its formative years, the leading political figures were also its leading intellectuals. Coeval with Jefferson, Franklin, and Adams further north, Carolina had its own leaders in these twin fields. The Pinckneys, Rutledges, and many others, it is true, were important because of their active careers in politics, and so belong properly to political history. But some Carolinians were distinguished more for their writings on the history and philosophy of government, hence are relevant to any broad cultural history.

The first eminent figure of this sort was a Philadelphian transplanted to Charleston in his early twenties, Dr. David Ramsay, whose writings during the first three decades of the young Republic — whether historical, political, or scientific — grew directly out of his commitment to Federalism and his ardent belief in the future of the new nation. Of his many historical works two are outstanding: *The Revolution in South Carolina* (1785) and his two volume *History of the American Revolution* (1789), which is regarded as the beginning of American historiography. Before the Revolution Charleston's intellectual life had been Europe-oriented; Ramsay's goal was to foster an American culture. In public orations, discussions at the Charleston Library Society (the hub of the city's intellectual life in the 1790's, but not in the 1990's!), and debates at the Literary and Philosophical Society, founded in 1813 just before his death, he vigorously promoted this new cultural nationalism. His goal seems even more inspiring by contrast with the diverse sectionalism which soon followed. My book must certainly reckon with David Ramsay.

My second choice of a dominant figure among Carolina's political authors must be, willy-nilly, John C. Calhoun. Born in the Upcountry and educated in New

England, he was torn between conflicting loyalties, national and sectional. Though he began as an ardent Federalist, defense of the South against antislavery forces gradually turned him in the other direction. During his lifetime his importance seemed to derive entirely from his brilliant political career: as U. S. Senator, cabinet officer, and vice-president — the leading Southern statesman. All of this put him outside my plan. But his reputation today is that of a political philosopher, a theorist of government, based though it is on two rather slender treatises. Completed at the end of his life, and near the terminal date of my book, his *Disquisition on Government* and the *Discourse on the Constitution* are central to all that Calhoun stood for. Though he failed to persuade his countrymen to put these theories into practice, they have continued to be influential on political thought not only in America but abroad. With the aid of a specialist colleague, I must reckon with Calhoun also.

When I turned to religious writings, or rather writings by clergymen, I was in for a series of surprises. Samuel Gilman, pastor of the Unitarian Church in Charleston, was the author of numerous poems and essays, the best of which he collected in a volume entitled *Contributions to Literature* (1856) — nothing that could properly be called religious. John Bachman, pastor of the Lutheran Church, was an even more prolific author, but the books he is most remembered for are in the field of science. Chief of these is the *Viviparous Quadrupeds of North America* in 3 volumes (1845-1848), in collaboration with J. J. Audubon, who supplied the plates while Bachman wrote the entire text. He was also a great help to Audubon in compiling the more famous Birds. His two books on religion are largely forgotten: *A Defense of Luther and the Reformation* (1853) and *The Unity of the Human Race* (1850), an effort to reconcile scripture with evolutionary theory. The most interesting book I found by an Episcopalian clergyman was the biggest surprise of all: *Philosophic Theology* (1849) by the Rev. J. W. Miles. Formerly a missionary in the Mid-East and afterwards a professor of philosophy at the College of Charleston, he was acquainted with religious thinkers from the Idealism of Plato to the Agnosticism of David Hume and the modern German Pantheists like Schelling, as well as with Christian, Buddhist, and Muslim scriptures. With this wide ranging background, he addressed his thesis to all those who "feel a difficulty in believing any system of Christianity except one which satisfies the exigencies of reason and science." But not really surprising, since the 18th century with its emphasis on logic and rational thought lingered on through the 19th in Charleston.

Taking the measure of such serious books, and others in similar non-literary categories, to see how I could utilize them in my cultural history — this occupied my morning work sessions for several weeks. Genie meanwhile was carrying on with her search through the endless heroic couplets that continued to pour forth from the pens of Charlestonians, à la Alexander Pope, one hundred years after his death! After four hours of such concentrated work we were more than ready for our lunch break. Salad and iced tea, fruit and some of Lucile's fresh baked biscuits, in our cool living/dining room. Then a real siesta, appropriate to this subtropical climate.

For our afternoon sessions we chose lighter work. One of the most pleasant was to go through again a number of excellent volumes we had skimmed last winter for a very different purpose, as guides to our sight-seeing. Anna Rutledge's book on the painters and Kitty Ravenel's on the native architects; then the professional studies of Charleston's dwelling houses and plantations by Stoney, Simons, and Lapham. This time a careful reading, with pencil and notebook in hand, to see how I could work into my cultural tapestry the riches made available to me by these experts on Charleston's artistic past. A bright thread of picturesque landscape or a telling portrait of some literary light; a classical structure in the Palladian or Georgian style for mansion or public building; the pattern of living aspired to by Charlestonians in the 18th and 19th centuries as revealed in the exteriors and interiors of the town houses and plantations they had commissioned. Would that all the work that goes into making a scholarly book were so enjoyable!

One larger pattern emerged from this re-reading. During the decades leading up to the Civil War, a building program was carried out in Charleston that "brilliantly transformed Meeting Street from an amorphous and largely vernacular group of buildings into an avenue of monumental high-style architecture," as the leading authority sums it up in an important new book (Kenneth Severens, *Charleston: Antebellum Architecture and Civic Destiny*, 1988). First to be built was Hibernian Hall in 1835, close copy of a Greek temple by a professional architect from Philadelphia. Then an eminent German architect, Charles Reichardt, was brought to Charleston, 1836-40, to design several public buildings, three of which were imposing Neoclassical structures. The Guard House (where the Post Office is now), with massive Doric colonnades; the Meeting Street Theater (site of two motor inns today), with a high portico of Ionic columns; and the Charleston Hotel covering a square city block on the grandest scale of all, with its facade of colossal Corinthian columns, boldly proclaiming Charleston's high destiny as "Queen of the South."

That dream was linked to several projects, including a new direct steamship line to Europe and a railroad system that would drain the trade of the Midwest through the port of Charleston. Though both projects collapsed a few years later, this resurgence of pride in its civic buildings set the tone of Charleston's aspirations for the next decade or two. Reichardt's monumental structures — together with the restrained Neoclassicism of Mill's Fireproof Building, the 18th century elegance of St. Michael's, the City Hall and Courthouse at the Four Corners of Law, and the Regency portico of Manigault's S. C. Society Hall — created a cityscape in a succession of classical styles for quarter of a mile along Meeting street "unmatched elsewhere in America," according to Severens. (Alas his book was not available fifty years ago!) As such, it was praised by Caroline Gilman in the *Southern Rose,* in the 1840s, and by another local author in a literary journal called *The Orion.* Perhaps this renaissance in architecture, the visual art for which Charleston is most noted, might serve as a paradigm for my history of its many sided cultural life during those momentous decades from 1830 to 1860. Even the fate of Reichardt's buildings — destroyed by the great fire of 1861, the earthquake of 1886, and neglect during the half century of economic ruin that followed 1865 — seem like mocking echoes of the disaster of Civil War that wrote "finis" to my proposed book. So much has perished that it is only by reading history, by searching through files of old lithographs and photos, that we today can realize the grandeur of ante-bellum Charleston's aspirations.

Thus our most pleasurable reading sessions brought substantial rewards. But they had to be spliced in with another more solemn undertaking. To read, or at least to skim, the whole shelf of William Gilmore Simm's writings: some forty novels and more than a dozen volumes of history and biography, not to mention his attempts at poetry. Making one's way through that literary wilderness was an achievement in itself, yet we managed it after a fashion before the summer was over. The best of his fiction is contained in about a dozen volumes: the romances of colonial and Indian life, and of the Revolutionary War, and the novels of frontier life in the South during the years of westward migration to the Mississippi. These we read with some real interest. Simms was the dominant literary figure in Charleston during the last three decades before the Civil War, yet something of an odd-man-out since he was the only professional man of letters in a culture of gentlemen amateurs. One more dilemma for me to reckon with.

Our afternoon sessions, whether wholly pleasurable or lightly serious, were followed by another dip in the ocean, preferably a bit of surf-boarding if the tide was bringing the rollers in. If not, we sometimes tried another kind of relaxing half hour, scrambling up the sand dunes wherever storm and flood had tossed them, thick with sea oats and palmetto fronds. Once in a while Lucile joined us in these wild walks, a city girl who was taking advantage of this opportunity to see a bit of Nature. Since she was "living in" this summer we had our main meal, dinner, at night, but we always finished in time for her to have the evening free with her beloved radio.

Occasionally I brought out my guitar after dinner, and we added a little music of our own to what the seaside night had to offer, never loud enough to disturb our neighbors. Genie had a bell-like ballad voice, and with me strumming an accompaniment she would sing one of her favorite old Scottish ballads:

When cockle shells turn silver bells
And mussels grow on every tree;
When blooms the rose 'neath wintry snows
Then will my love be true to me.

Or we'd give voice together in one of those slightly bawdy ballads from the Southern Mountains:

On the top of Old Smokey
All covered with snow,
There I lost my true lover
Through a'courting too slow.

Or a spiritual, softly hummed. More often than not, as on our first evening at Folly Beach, we'd prefer listening to the natural music of wind and wave, before turning in for a good night's sleep.

Once again our way of life settled into a routine so smooth that the tick of the calendar clock drifted into a kind of timelessness, and we lost track of days and weeks. Our looting of the past for its treasures went on a-pace, with occasional unexpected finds. Our periods of pure pleasure — well, Genie had learned to swim, what more need be said? We were busy and healthy and happy in a natural habitat, however simple, a place of peace and privacy. Even the most mundane aspect of living, keeping the larder full, was an agreeable part of the pattern. Once or twice a week Genie drove Lucile several miles up the Folly Road to the little stands where they bought our supplies. To the docks for seafood: local favorites like porgies, or sheepshead and red snapper from out beyond the harbor. These we could alternate with chicken or country ham, but for other meats we had to wait for trips into town. A variety of fresh vegetables were available: peas and beans, okra and tomatoes; no sweet corn in the South in those days except Country Gentleman, which would do for fritters but not on-the-cob; occasionally some tasty young mustard greens and, as a surprise, a kind of wild asparagus called locally "cheney-briar" or "poke-weed." The seasonal fruits went from berries to peaches to figs, giving us some inkling that time was moving on. We fared well, in a country sort of way. And Sam Stoney dropped in for dinner several times, though not as often as promised. The blissful sequence of our days began to remind us of that old lady's dream, but there was nothing monotonous about our paradise. New ideas and new challenges surfaced almost every day from our deep diving into ante-bellum Charleston.

10

Gala Interlude

One of the best ways to appreciate an ideal pattern of living is to have the pattern broken, temporarily. This perspective enhances the value of what is being missed, while at the same time giving reassurance that the ideal way will be restored soon. And if the event that breaks the pattern is in its own way a pleasurable one, so much the better. This is what happened to us during the first week of August, just past the half-way mark of our summer at Folly Beach. Genie's Aunt Dolly and Uncle Walter Lamar drove over from Macon, bringing my parents along, for a brief visit. They arrived in mid afternoon after a comfortable trip, with her renowned chauffeur Henry at the wheel. Aunt Dolly always did things with a flourish, so the first thing to appear from the capacious trunk of the Cadillac was a hamper packed with everything needed for a picnic supper: fried chicken, salad, a homemade loaf, and a bushel basket of choice Georgia peaches. Our beach house had plenty of bedrooms to accommodate all, including an extra one on the ground floor for Henry — a married man, but not averse to a little holiday dalliance. Lucile's slender

good looks and knowing city ways soon had him danc-
ing, and she found his special style entertaining to
say the least. So this aspect of the two day visit was
all wrapped up from the start. They functioned beau-
tifully as a team, though there was one near-mishap.

Before sitting down to our sumptuous supper they
all wanted to have a go at beach life, the sky being
overcast so there was no danger of freckles or blis-
ters. Auntie and Gertrude donned their Gibson Girl
bathing costumes and sat on the beach, where they
could dabble their toes in the water at high tide. Robbie joined me on the surf boards, a new experience, but
I was proud of him for the skill and courage with
which he set about learning at nearly seventy years
of age. Uncle Walter tried the side stroke down to the
old stump with Genie. But our guests did not come to
Folly for beach life. This was a family gathering, and
we sat on the porch long into the evening catching
up on all the news, an occupation that continued for
much of the next day.

Dinner on the second evening was to be *our* party,
and we had placed an order in advance for soft-shelled
crabs as our centerpiece. But the main attraction was
to be Sam Stoney, who promised to drive down and
bring Anna Rutledge with him.

"I hope you've brought your white coat," Genie said
to Henry. "This is to be a real party, not like the picnic last night, and Lucile will have on her best."

Henry was a man of many parts: expert chauffeur,

butler with a flourish, and general factotum for Aunt Dolly ("I do most of her thinking for her"). But he was also skilful at slipping out of things. "I declare, Miss Eugenia, looks like I just clean forgot to bring that white coat." Genie, convinced this was not an accident, said that was too bad; he'd just have to take care of everything in the kitchen, and Lucile would do the serving. All seemed agreeably settled, but as the day wore on it threatened to get unsettled. Gert and Rob began regaling the Lamars, especially at lunch time, with an account of Stoney the raconteur, his spicy anecdotes mixed with genealogy, and his tall-tales of pseudo-history from the odd corners of old Charleston. Henry began to suspect that he was going to miss a great treat, so he put in another plea. "Miss Eugenia, just lemme sort of hover out there helping a little, where I can hear but not mostly be seen." But she wouldn't yield.

It turned out to be just the right kind of summer evening for dining on the porch, after a mint julep. Neither the Lamars nor my parents were given to alcoholic beverages, but they couldn't decline the traditional ones. Back in the kitchen Henry was adept at crushing the ice and stirring until the juleps were properly frosted, but it was Lucile who served them. As the stories got under way, and the laughter followed, poor Henry became almost frantic. When he had done sufficient penance for his sin of forgetting, Genie put a word in Uncle Walter's ear and he slipped out unnoticed to the bedroom. A few minutes later Henry appeared resplendent in a borrowed Palm Beach coat, serving the first course in his inimitable style.

I suppose our guests enjoyed the dinner part of that evening — we had put our best culinary foot forward, Folly Beach style — but all else fades from memory except Sam's performance. With several new pairs of ears in his audience, he was in top form. It's quite impossible to recapture the wit, the actor's skills, and the spontaneous responses of a captive audience that makes such an evening memorable. Maybe just a condensed version of Sam's famous Gullah sermon on the Creation, which he saved for his after dinner climax:

"What you moanin' for down there in that gyarden, Adam?"

"I just lonely. Nobody to play with down here. I wants me a woman, or something."

"Adam, that moanin' of yours 'bout to drive me crazy. I'm tired of creatin', but 'spect I'll have to come back down in that Eden of yours and shape up some sort of Eve."

The Lord he workin' round there most of that day, trying to shape up that mud. "Take your Barlow knife, Adam, and go out there in the bushes and bring some stout twigs to hold this stuff together." Then the Lord look up and see the sun going down.

"Quittin' time," he said. "Have to finish this woman tomorrow."

We slept late the next day, recovering from our gala evening.

The morning after our party we passed in leisurely style, a short walk on the beach, a long sit and talk on the porch before their departure about noon. They were planning to break the drive back to Georgia by an overnight stop in Charleston with Mrs. Andrew Geer, one of Aunt Dolly's colleagues on the Board of Directors at Stratford, Robert E. Lee's birthplace on the Potomac. She led a full and active life, taking an important part in civic affairs and national projects related to history. She had the imagination and the dynamic drive. Uncle Walter supplied the money, and they made an effective team. But it would be misleading to imply that Aunt Dolly was a bossy busybody. She was a lady of great charm and wit, as may be illustrated by a brief anecdote which I will borrow from an event that happened about ten years later. Her crowning ambition was to become President of the United Daughters of the Confederacy. Fancying herself as something of an orator, she prepared her inaugural address with great care. As she reached her peroration "...who was the noblest knight of the *ancien regime*...who led his country as bravely in defeat as in victory...who stands first in the hearts of his people," then a pause for maximum effect. What followed was the classic slip-of-the-tongue for all time.

Not Jefferson Davis, but ABRAHAM LINCOLN! Aunt Dolly made the front cover of *Time*, and nobody enjoyed the fiasco more than she.

11

End Of An Era,
And A Year

The visit of our Georgia family was a most diverting interlude. But it was surprising how quickly we re-established our old routine of learning about Charleston's past and swimming at Folly Beach in the present, so that there hardly seemed to have been a break in our summer way of life. But this pattern was drifting to a close. Even idylls do not last forever. Though there was still much ground to cover in the way of reading and research, I began to think about plans for handling all this disparate material. To shape it into a book, I must develop a thesis that would indicate what to emphasize and what to skimp or skip altogether. First of all to decide on a struc-ture. A chronological narrative seemed not only log-ical but unavoidable, the historical development being echoed by shifts in the cultural pattern. There was clearly a Revolutionary period, followed by a Federal or Nationalist one, then the rise of Sectionalism to the climax of Secession and war. Not being a trained historian, I would confine myself to shifts in the cul-tural pattern, against a mere backdrop of historical facts borrowed from the best secondary sources. But like all simple plans it ran into complications almost from the outset.

I had assumed that since Charleston's culture was British-oriented during the first half of my century (1760-1860), I would find a culture of gentlemen amateurs rather than professionals. But the exceptions loomed large. As early as 1800 three of the most talented Charlestonians had opted for professional careers, and before the age of twenty-one had deserted their native shores for an urban world richer in opportunities for their chosen fields. Washington Allston, the painter, went to London; Robert Mills, architect, to Washington, where he designed many government buildings including the Washington Monument (though he did return to South Carolina as state architect for a decade, 1820-1830, designing amongst other masterpieces Charleston's classical Fireproof Building); and John Izard Middleton, archeologist, who moved to Rome, where he wrote *Grecian Remains in Italy*, illustrated with his own drawings. All won wider reputations than would have been likely had they remained as gentlemen amateurs in Charleston.

As the nineteenth century moved on, the national spirit in America inspired authors and intellectuals generally to attempt professional careers. There was much talk about this in the reviews and journals published in Charleston also, but the cult of amateurism lingered on in this old fashioned city. When to that handicap was added a growing threat of sectionalism, other talented professionals chose to leave Charleston. By 1830, the halfway point in my ante-bellum period, the playwright and literary editor Isaac Harby had decamped to New York. A few years later there was a much greater loss. Hugh Swinton Legare, learned editor of the *Southern Review*, discouraged by the failure of Charlestonians to support this ambitious journal and agonized as a Unionist by the rabid sectionalism of the Nullification Movement, happily accepted the post of Minister to Belgium to escape the heat of controversy, 1832-1836, then spent his last years in Washington as Congressman and U. S. Attorney General, more honored by his country than by his native city.

One more example, at the very end of the ante-bellum period. Basil Gildersleeve, one of several Charlestonians attracted by the prestige of German universities, took his Ph. D. in Classical Studies at Göttingen. Though there were a surprising number of amateur classicists in Charleston, also in Beaufort and Columbia, Gildersleeve was determined on a professional career. He left his birthplace in 1856 to become professor of Greek at the University of Virginia (then, in the decades after the Civil War, as the influential classicist at Johns Hopkins University). The South continued to lead the nation in Greek and Latin scholarship right down to 1860, while New England was pioneering the study of modern European languages and literatures. One more bit of evidence that the South was old fashioned, even at the peak of its ante-bellum prosperity! This has been put with bravura by Stoney in his introduction to the Octagon Library volume *Charleston*. During the period of Charleston's greatest importance, he says, from 1769 right on down to 1860, the city and its people remained essentially of the 18th century: "It was then that their culture crystallized. Their mode of thought, their institutions, and their very pronunciation keep the flavor of that age. From that time they preserved the tradition of the classic, with its intellectual freedom, its moral tolerance, its discipline in matters of etiquette, its individualism, and the spirit of logic which elsewhere largely perished in the romantic movement."

Gilmore Simms, the tireless advocate of professionalism in literature, remained in Charleston complaining to the end about the way, in this planter-dominated society, authorship was slighted "as the work of the amateur, a labor of stealth or recreation, employed as a relief from other more important tasks and duties." Gentlemen amateurs or professionals? There was no simple line of development that characterized ante-bellum Charleston's culture in this respect. But certainly the movement from a Nationalist orientation in the early decades of the young republic to the Sectionalism dominating the years from 1830 to 1860 did seem to offer a straight line narrative that could give structure to my book. Once again, the simple solution began to show complications. Not just in the occasional pro-Southerner who spoke out in the early 1800's, or the odd Unionist like James Louis Petigru who marched out of St. Michael's Church when the U.S. flag was removed in 1861! Complications much harder to unravel. When the spirit of Sectionalism first developed, the emphasis in literature and other intellectual activities was on celebrating in a positive way the unique culture that Charleston and the South had to offer the young nation. But as the attacks of Abolitionists and other Northern critics of the slavery system were stepped up, Southern writers became more and more defensive. Such a stance was more likely to produce propaganda than literature.

My thinking was not bringing solutions but unearthing more problems. At first I was discouraged at not finding a simple structure for organizing my materials. Then I realized that a cultural history dramatized by controversy, and enriched by paradoxes and ambiguities, would be much more interesting than a simple story of an old-fashioned Charleston that would have merely elicited some banality such as "picturesque" or "charming." I didn't have a solution, but I did have some dilemmas to cope with. In coping with them, I hoped to formulate a thesis that would unify my book. Rather, a series of interlocking theses, since my dilemmas were clearly inter-related. Reluctantly I began to face the possibility that the

Old Slave Mart

(Watercolor by Paul Hogarth, R.A.)

South's "peculiar institution," the whole system of plantation slavery, was the link, the common denominator of my several dilemmas. Reluctantly, because I still feared my cultural history would get lost in that controversy; besides, this was a field I had no competence in whatever. The whole problem would have to wait until I returned to Duke University where I could lay out these voluminous notes in my study and where one of my colleagues, a specialist in ante-bellum Southern history, could advise me how to keep the cultural and political issues separated as far as possible, the latter relegated to the background.

Back now to our problem of reading and note-taking, which continued right on until the end of our Folly Island summer. The passage of time during a working-holiday, in an island paradise dedicated to activity rather than idleness, can best be indicated by its vanishing. Days simply disappeared and weeks went by uncounted.

One of our last major projects was to go through the whole file of *Russell's Magazine* (1857-1860), Charleston's most celebrated literary journal, which brought to a climax the most brilliant decade in the city's intellectual life. This monthly, devoted largely to current literature and ideas, was in striking contrast to Charleston's best journal of an earlier period, Legare's *Southern Review* (1828-1832), a quarterly filled with learned essays on the classics and the masterpieces of British literature. More to the point would be a comparison with the *Atlantic Monthly*, launched the same year, 1857, by the literati of New England. *Russell's* was consciously begun as a rival, promoted by the group of authors and intellectuals who met as an informal club in the back room of Russell's Bookstore, the cultural elite of the city who also formed the corps of contributors.

Simms was the doyen of this group, presiding over its gatherings like another Dr. Johnson. (Leader of the South's vanguard in the 1850's still enamored of the eighteenth century!) Magisterially he gave the nod to his protégé Paul Hayne by appointing him editor of *Russell's Magazine*. Comparison with the *Atlantic* is instructive, also a bit distressing. The Boston magazine had a much larger pool of authors to draw on, many of them already established as professionals like Hawthorne, Emerson, and Lowell, and a much larger circle of subscribers to give it financial backing. Despite all this, Charleston's monthly at its best offered brave competition during its few years of life. The dreams of literary glory indulged in by Simms' little coterie were aborted by the new wave of sectionalism that swept the South when Lincoln was nominated for the presidency. *Russell's Magazine* collapsed a few months before South Carolina took the lead in a very different direction, Secession from the Union on 20 December 1860. Less than four months later Confederate forces fired on Fort Sumter, guns that signalled the beginning of the Civil War —

and the terminal date of my cultural history of ante-bellum Charleston.

Deeply engrossed as we were, reading about the build-up to that disastrous war and cut off by choice in our island retreat from outside news and noise, we actually did not learn about the outbreak of World War II until several days after 3 September 1939, when we bought a newspaper on our weekly trip into town!

Time now to wind up our summer idyll, indeed our whole wonderful Charleston year. Doubly sad for Genie who had been brought up on the water, in Baltimore and California, and had taken great joy in the ocean at Folly Beach and along the harbor in the city. As for our happy life in lovely old Charleston and our friendships there, we kept the parting cheerful by endless promises to come back. (And come back we did, before many months elapsed.) Our special friends came to the island for a swim, for lunch or drinks. The older ones we paid a call on during trips to the Library Society to return books, or to help Lucile make the transition back to her own rooms in the city. That parting really brought tears. Otherwise we avoided saying goodbye. Instead, in all the languages we could muster — *au revoir, auf Wiedersehen, arrivederci* — Charleston, here we come again!

12

Departure (And Return)

Almost the first thing I did after leaving Charleston and going back to my post at Duke University in mid-September was to set in motion a plan for renewing the Charleston connection. A conference with colleagues in Art and History resulted in an invitation being sent to Samuel Gaillard Stoney to give a lecture to staff and students of these two departments on the "Architecture of Old Charleston," with a modest fee to cover expenses. (They had been impressed by his book on the *Plantations*.) I wrote a letter at the same time inviting him to be our guest, so he could pocket most of the fee. Early in November he drove up to Durham.

The formal afternoon lecture, with slides of the town houses as well as plantations, brought out a good audience which Sam held in the palm of his hand by his professional expertise combined with a lively stage presence. But the high point of his visit came that evening. We had invited a few friends in the English Department for a buffet supper, with a dozen more to come afterwards for an informal talk by Sam on the Gullah language. The guests were just arriving when the telephone rang. It was Sue Myrick, my old journalist friend from Macon, just back from California where she had been coaching Vivien Leigh and Clark Gable for proper Georgia accents in their roles as Scarlett and Rhett Butler in *Gone With the Wind*, so as to avoid that phony Hollywood notion of Southern speech. Sue and Sam, two stars in one small living room! Both of them were skilful raconteurs, hence monologuists eager for the ears of auditors. Eugenia and I sat back and let them battle it out. Gable's gaffes and Vivien's Anglo-Southern hybrids mimicked by Sue. Adam and Eve in that Gyarden by Parson Stoney. Hard to say who enjoyed that evening the most, audience or performers.

Several months after Sam returned to Charleston he worked out another way of keeping our connections going. As President of the Poetry Society of South Carolina, Sam wrote me, he had suggested to the committee for choosing the annual speaker that since they'd had such a poor success recently by inviting celebrities, "Why not invite somebody no one has ever heard of?" They agreed. "How about it, Charles, will you come?" Later Sam gave me an example of their celebrity flops. The speaker last year was St. John Gogarty, author and wit, whose reminiscences of his friends in the Irish literary Renaissance had just been published. On the platform, with too many shots of Jameson's under his belt, he began to stumble a bit, then to mumble: "Well, there was Leonardo and his supper party, and Michelangelo painting the ceiling of his sister's chapel, and all that ..." Sam had to touch his shoulder and whisper, "Irish, not Italian Renaissance."

My response to Sam's inverted flattery was a resounding, "I'll come." The fee of $100 almost took my breath away.

In April we made our pilgrimage to the Holy City. During the six months we'd been back at Duke I had shaped up my research materials to the point where I was able to draft a lecture on "Gentlemen Amateurs in Ante-bellum Charleston" that would be a kind of preview of my proposed book. The annual meeting of the Poetry Society of South Carolina in those days was a black tie affair, held in 1940 at the Dock Street Theater if my memory is not playing me a stage trick. Sam gave me the perfect introduction: a warm welcome tempered by wit. Then I did the unthinkable. I launched into a lecture on Charleston's cultural history before a local audience all of whom already knew what Charleston's history was "really" like. I bearded the Lowcountry lion (lioness) in his (her) lair and came out unscathed! Afterwards our special friends had been invited to the Stoney's home on Tradd Street, where in his garden Sam served us his favorite West Indian rum punch: One of strong and two of weak, one of sour and two of sweet. For the Andersons it was a wonderful evening all round, a kind of reunion and memorial celebration of our sabbatical year in

Charleston.

(P.S. Nearly half a century later there has been a resurgence of historical writings on South Carolina, spear-headed by the state's premier historian George Rogers. One of these is especially relevant here: a volume of nearly 500 pages entitled *Intellectual Life in Antebellum Charleston* (1986), edited by Michael O'Brien and David Moltke-Hansen and contributed to by a dozen specialists. Even this large scale undertaking covers only a part of the field that I, in my innocence, was planning to encompass in my Cultural History of Ante-bellum Charleston. Some *genius loci*, wiser than I, must have presided over the destiny of my proposed book, realizing that it was much more than I could cope with alone.)

Shortly after giving my talk before the Poetry Society a major change came in my professional life. I was invited to join the English faculty of Johns Hopkins University. Part of the package was that I would have the first year free of teaching duties in order to begin work on a ten volume edition of the works and letters of Sidney Lanier. The poet's family had donated their large collection of manuscripts, on condition that I should be editor-in-chief. This meant that my Charleston book must be laid aside for a while, just as the biography of Paul Hayne had been sidetracked by Melville a decade before. In the event, the Lanier Edition took me five gruelling years to finish. After that, one thing led to another, that is, one writing project after another took possession of my pen, declining to be gainsaid. As a result, the Poetry Society lecture on "Gentlemen Amateurs in Ante-bellum Charleston," intended as only a preview of my Cultural History of Ante-bellum Charleston, turned out to be the only view of it to see the light of day. Every author, I suppose, has one book that he feels especially tender about — the book he never got around to writing!

The Way It Is, Now

Charleston has apparently been "in my stars" from birth. At any rate, here I am back in Charleston, fifty years later, not in a rented house on Elliott Street but in our own home on Legare Street, permanently. The first phase of my life came to an end with the untimely death of Eugenia Blount. The second phase began when I married Mary Pringle Fenhagen, widow of a prominent Baltimore architect. The Pringle family have been established Charlestonians for over two hundred and fifty years, actively involved in preservation for several generations. Mary's grandmother saved from demolition the old Powder Magazine, her mother the Joseph Manigault House. She was also a co-founder of the Preservation Society in 1920.

After my retirement from Johns Hopkins University and Mary's from the Enoch Pratt Library, we challenged Thomas Wolfe's dictum "You Can't Go Home Again" by moving back to her native Charleston. From the vantage ground of 4 Legare Street, with Mary's splendid library of South Caroliniana at our elbow, we have watched with growing concern the unprecedented changes taking place during the last two decades. Some of them have threatened to transform Charleston — a lovely old city where families could live peacefully in a traditional community — into a tourist mecca surrounded by a chain of island resorts. This raises again the question I began with. Can Charleston, as well as Paris boast:

La plus ça change, la plus c'est la même chose?

Fifty years ago the tourist "season" lasted only a month or so, during the camellia and azalea flowering in the great gardens. And it drew just a few thousand visitors. Today, tourists pour into the Lowcountry throughout the year, with some seasonal ebbings and floodings, but adding up to nearly five million annually. And the Chamber of Commerce adds proudly, "They spend almost a billion dollars!"

What price prosperity? A steady erosion of the peaceful world, the quiet communal life, the gentle manners of yesterday. The streets of Charleston are bustling all day long. At peak hours — with the tour buses, guided groups of walkers, the noisy harangues of tourist carriage drivers — traffic slows down bumper to bumper, or bumper to horses' tails.

Many Charlestonians, old and young, have sold their houses or despaired of ever acquiring one and fled across the Ashley and Cooper Rivers, to escape from the buzz of tourism and the wild escalation of taxes and property prices. The old residential area is filled with clamor and its streets jammed with moving vans and restorers' trucks as houses change hands constantly, because of the bull market in real estate. Some of the grand-scale mansions have been bought by absentee owners, some have been turned into deluxe inns, a half-dozen are "museum houses." Many smaller ones are now bed-and-breakfast places. These changes may help to save fine old houses. But what price preservation?

As the new prosperity has increased, the residential population of the old peninsular city has actually shrunk. At the same time, the flood of newcomers, augmented by refugees from the peninsula, have turned "West of the Ashley" and "East of the Cooper" into sprawling suburban areas two or three times as populous as the old city, where a sense of community and the Charleston way of life are hard to come by. One by one, department stores and the like, which supplied the daily needs of Charlestonians, have moved to shopping centers and malls ten miles out in the country. Their places on King and Meeting Streets are now occupied by shops that cater to a transient trade, selling everything from souvenir trinkets to luxury items.

"The more it changes, the more it's the same thing?" It is essential that Charleston should realize how fragile her grandeur is! Vulnerable not only to the ravages of nature — hurricane, earthquake, fire and flood — but to the hazards posed by progress. The

Board of Architectural Review has long been the watchdog of Charleston's splendid architectural heritage. But what board or committee stands guard over her less visible but equally important heritage: the concern for privacy, peace, and manners that make up Charleston's unique way-of-life?

There have been many encouraging activities in Charleston during these last two decades, of course. Notably those sponsored by three venerable organizations established for the purpose of preserving Old Charleston rather than transforming it. Historic Charleston Foundation, a highly effective non-profit organization with the ingenious use of a revolving fund, has rescued whole sections of the city, such as Ansonborough, from decay. The expanding activity of the South Carolina Historical Society, now housed in the handsome Fireproof Building, is filling its archives with valuable manuscripts and all manner of historical records of Charleston and the whole of Carolina. And the revitalized Preservation Society soldiers on into its second half century. Long may they all flourish!

There also seems to be promise of another cultural renaissance. Quite a few impressive new talents have appeared on the scene recently in literature and art. Novelists, poets, painters, authors of illustrated books on the Lowcountry, and scholarly historians — mostly natives, but with some healthy infusion from outside. And especially in music and the performing arts, culminating in the famous Spoleto Festival every summer. Authentic Old Charleston is showing signs of new life. Maybe it will survive after all, and not be transformed beyond all recognition!

The Author

Charles Anderson was educated at the University of Georgia and at Columbia University, where he took a Ph.D. in English. The climax of his teaching career was the thirty years at Johns Hopkins University, where he was the Caroline Donovan Professor of American Literature. He is the author of more than a dozen books, including major studies of Emily Dickinson and Henry James, both of which won the Phi Beta Kappa Prize for literary criticism.

He served as visiting professor at Heidelberg (1949), the University of Rome (1952 - 1953), and the Nagano Seminar in Japan (1955). After retirement he served as USIS lecturer in American Literature at universities in more than twenty-five countries throughout Europe and Asia. The academic life is not necessarily spent in an Ivory Tower!

The Andersons divide the year between Charleston and Cambridge, England.

The Illustrator

Paul Hogarth is a Royal Academician and an eminent British painter and illustrator. His two most recent books are: *Graham Greene Country*, illustrations for that shelf of famous English novels; and *The Mediterranean Shore*, paintings for the fiction and travel books of Lawrence Durell, who has praised Hogarth's watercolors for their "blithe and tender line, backed up with seraphic colouring." Hogarth's earlier books include three travel guides to historic Boston, Philadelphia, and Washington. In 1984, during a visit to Charleston, he painted a number of watercolors of this historic city, four of which are reproduced in the present book, with his kind permission.